Peter Harrison's
PC Crash Course Series

MICROSOFT® WORD
for Windows™ v6

GW00500516

Thank you for buying this product from **PC Productions Limited**, and welcome to our fast growing user-group. We hope that you will be fully satisfied with this course, and also enjoy using it.

PC Productions Limited does not provide any guarantees whatsoever regarding the contents of this course and reserves the right to make improvements and/or changes in the course, or any accompanying materials, whenever necessary or advisable. Any error in content or typography will be corrected in the next edition.

Printed and bound in Great Britain by
Cromwell Press Limited.

PC Productions Limited, Kendrick Hall, Kendrick St,
STROUD, GL5 1AA. U.K. Tel (0453) 755200.

ISBN 1 873005 24-5

Your exercise diskette

The diskette that accompanies this course contains the files you will need to follow the exercises in the course. <u>You will find instructions on how to use your diskette as you progress through the manual</u>.

There is no need to install the diskette on your computer.

Conventions used in the course

To make it easier to understand and use this course we have used different typefaces as explained below.

Instructions

Instructions are preceded by a dot, e.g.:

- Make sure your printer is switched on and ready to go.

Items that you are to type on the keyboard are printed in a different typeface and indented, e.g.:

- Type:

  Type this now!

Whenever specific keys, buttons or options are referred to, we print the item in bold type, as follows:

- Press the **Enter** key,

or,

- Click **OK**.

Key combinations

Key combinations are sometimes referred to with a plus sign between two keys. This means that the two keys should be pressed together, e.g.:

- Press **Shift+F8**

If two keys are separated by a comma then the keys should be pressed one after the other, e.g.:

- Press **Home**, **ArrowDown**.

General points

Items making a general point, which are not instructions to carry out immediately, are shown as follows:

  You could also have used the **Print Preview** feature.

Screen text

Items that refer to something displayed on your screen are shown under-lined or in a separate frame, e.g.

This is text that appears on your screen.

or,

```
This is displayed on your screen
```

Notes

Notes providing information to be remembered are shown as follows:

 *If you make a mistake typing in the text, use the **Backspace** key to delete the letter you just typed.*

Notes about learning

 It is a very good idea to make your own notes as you progress. Actually going through the process of making notes and summarizing your thoughts will help you to remember.

Always try to complete the chapter you are working with rather than breaking off in the middle.

There is no doubt that experimentation will help you learn. At the end of each chapter, feel free to experiment on your own. The further through the course you get, the more confidence you will gain. That's when you should start experimenting.

Quick Reference

Table of Contents

Contents

Contents

Contents

Contents

Introduction

The sheer volume of original documentation supplied with any major software application these days can be rather daunting to the somewhat inexperienced user. This course does not intend to simply replace that original documentation. However, the intention is to guide you through the most important features of the program, using language that is easy to understand and examples that are easy to follow. By the time you turn the last page of this course you will have become a reasonably sophisticated user of the program.

What is a word processing program?

A word processing program enables you to write letters, reports, memoranda, invoices and much, much more, quickly and efficiently. It will also enable you to print them out and store them for future reference, editing or alteration.

Your word processing system (program plus computer) could be considered to be a typewriter equipped with built-in scissors, paste and correction fluid - a typewriter that is designed to function as a copier as well! This means that you will never have to rewrite a page because it contains an error. You'll simply correct the error. If you want to send the same letter to a number of different people, you can do this quickly and effectively by copying the letter as many times as required and inserting the different names and addresses.

Generally speaking, a word processing program functions in the same way as a highly sophisticated typewriter. You don't have to interrupt your work in any way when a line fills up or at the end of a page. The program automatically advances your text onto a new line or new page. Thanks to the many different print styles available - particularly if you have a laser printer connected to the system - you can create professional, attractively styled letters and other documents.

What can a word processing package do?

Here is a list of things that you can expect to do with a major word processing package. Not all features are necessarily available with your word processing program, nor are all the features covered in this course.

New	You can type in new documents from scratch.
Save	You can save your documents on your hard disk, or on a diskette.
Open	You can retrieve your documents from your hard disk or diskette to use them again.
Edit	You can change a document as much as you want to.
Format	You can apply different formats to your text, such as **bold** type, *italics*, <u>underlining</u>, etc. You can also align paragraphs.
Move	You can move blocks of text around in your document, or between different documents, using a feature often known as 'cut and paste'. You may also get a 'drop and drag' feature to allow you to move text around with the mouse.
Print	You can print out a document as many times as you wish to.
Tables	You can design tables quickly and easily.
Page layout	You can set up the page layout - paper size, margins, etc.
Spell check	You can check specific words or whole documents against an 'electronic' dictionary.
Thesaurus	You can look up synonyms (words with similar meanings) for any word.
Grammar	You can check for grammatical errors.
Auto-save	You can set your program up to automatically save the document you are working with - say every 15 mins.
Mail merge	You can set up a document file containing a standard letter and a data file containing names and addresses, and merge the two to create a series of personalised letters.

Addresses	You can often quickly address envelopes, or print address labels.
WYSIWYG	'What You See Is What You Get' pronounced wizzy-wig! You see the document on screen with all its enhancements.
Print preview	Allows you to see a complete page exactly as it will be printed on your printer.
Macros	Macros allow you to record keystrokes for common tasks, or even often repeated phrases. Each macro can then be replayed to automate that task. In time, you could build up some very complex macros.
Indexes	You can generate indexes and tables of contents.
Graphics	You can import graphics produced in other software packages and add them to your document.
Import	You can load text from other software packages into your document.
Export	Your documents can be used in other software packages.

Other features

Word for Windows also has some other features to help you on your way. These incluse AutoFormat, AutoCorrect, AutoText and Wizards, all of which are covered in this course.

With so much to learn, it's time to get started! ***GOOD LUCK!***

Getting Started

In this chapter you will learn how to start your Microsoft Word program, and how to select items from its menu system. It is assumed that you have installed the program.

Starting Word

- Switch on your computer and printer.

- Start Windows.

To start Word you doubleclick the Microsoft Word icon which is in the **Word for Windows 6.0** group window, unless this was changed when the program was installed. If you are running **Microsoft Office**, it may be in the Microsoft Office group window.

- If the group window containing the Word icon is not already open, doubleclick on it to open it.

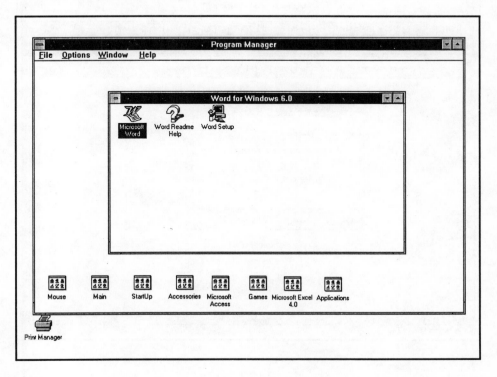

☞ *All the pictures in this course are from an SVGA screen (800 x 600) on a system running Windows for Workgroups 3.1. Your screen displays may differ slightly to the pictures shown, but the important details will be the same.*

You can now start the Word program by doubleclicking its icon.

- Doubleclick the **Microsoft Word** program icon.

Your Microsoft Word program should now start.

☞ *If you are presented with the Quick Preview screen, click the* **Return to Word** *button. You can run the Quick Preview at any time by selecting it from the Help menu.*

Tip of the day

The *Tip of the Day* feature simply gives you different tips on how to use Word more effectively. Each time you start Word, a new tip will be displayed.

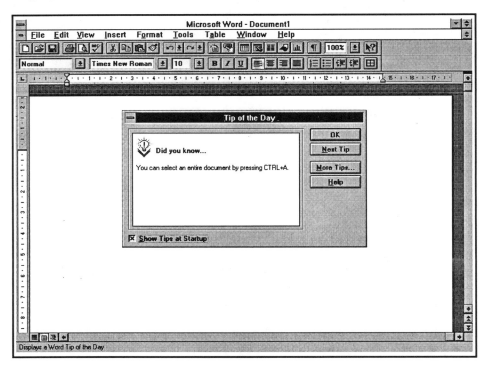

It can be quite useful to read these tips and gradually 'soak in' useful information about working with Word. At some later point, but not just now, you could choose to do one of the following:

☺ Click on **More Tips**, to show another tip.

☺ Click on the **Show Tips at Startup** option, so that it is not crossed, to stop Word from showing the tips when you start it.

● For now, just click **OK**, to close the Tip of the Day dialog box.

The document window

The main document window is displayed and its most important features are named in the picture below.

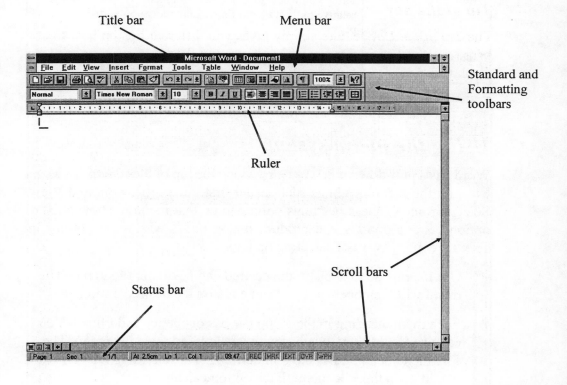

The table on the following page explains the main areas.

Area	*Description*
Title bar	Displays 'Microsoft Word' and the current document name.
Menu bar	Consists of a list of menus that can be opened to select features and functions.
Standard toolbar	Short cut buttons to quickly access some features by clicking on the button.
Formatting toolbar	Short cut buttons to help you quickly change the format of the text.
Ruler	Ruler to help you judge positions and quickly set tabs, etc.
Text area	Area for writing your document.
Scroll bars	Show you whereabouts in the document you are working, relative to its start and finish, and allow you to display other pages.
Status bar	Displays information about the active document or selected feature.

Using the menu system

Word has a pull-down menu system. Along the top of the screen is a Menu bar with the menu headings such as the first three; File, Edit, and View. Selecting one of these headings will open up that menu to show a list of options. Some options will produce dialog boxes with more options in. There are many ways of selecting options.

- Use the mouse to click on the desired choice on the Menu bar. The menu will then open and you can click on the desired option.

- Each menu heading in the menu bar has one letter underlined. You can use the **Alt** key together with this letter to open the menu. The **File** menu heading has the F underlined. Thus pressing **Alt+F** would open the **File** menu. Each option can also be chosen by then pressing the corresponding underlined or highlighted letter for that option.

⊛ Some options have a short cut key combination, such as **Ctrl+S** to save the current document. You will learn some of these combinations as you go through the course.

⊛ Many options have a button on the toolbar that allow you to quickly select the option. If you position the mouse pointer over a button on the toolbar, a small box will be shown below the button to tell you what it does.

⊛ In a dialog box, you will often see one option is active by a dotted line around that option. This means that pressing **Enter** will cause the active option to be selected. You can use the **Tab** key to move between the various options on display.

The method you eventually choose will be a personal decision. Most people combine the different methods in a natural way to work most effectively.

Using the mouse

You will now try selecting one of the menu options using the mouse.

- Click on the **View** option in the Menu bar to open the View menu.

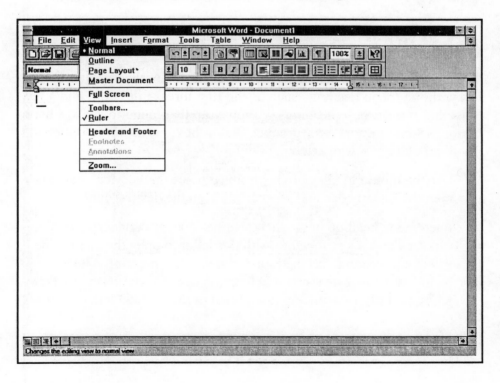

The View menu is now open and some of the options can be selected. Here are a few points to note:

⊕ The options shown in a lighter shade are not available at the present moment and cannot be selected.

⊕ Some options have three dots after them, e.g. **Toolbars...** this means that selecting the option will produce a dialog box.

⊕ Some options will have a tick to their left, e.g. the **Ruler** option, this is used for options that can be turned on and off by selecting the option. A tick means that the option is on, or active.

⊕ Some options will have a dot to their left, e.g. ● **Normal**, this is used to show which option from a group of options is selected, or active.

⊕ Some options will have a short cut key combination to their right, e.g. **Save   Ctrl+S** (in the File menu). These key combinations can be used without first having to open the menu to be selected.

● Click on the **Zoom** option.

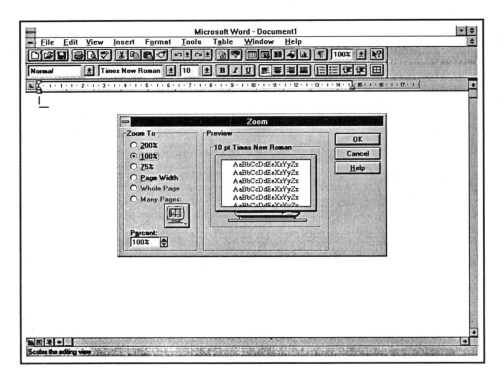

The Zoom dialog box is now displayed. Don't worry about what it all means for now, you will just close it again.

• Click on **Cancel**.

Using the short cut buttons

Some of the menu options have a short cut button in the toolbar or ribbon. The example to the left is the short cut button to start the spelling checker program.

• Position the mouse pointer over the **Spelling** button in the toolbar, without clicking on it, and wait a second - a small box that names the button will show that you are pointing at the **Spelling** button.

• Click the **Spelling** button.

Because the document is empty, the spelling check will be over straight away.

• Click on **OK**.

☞ *Just in case!*
If, for some reason, you have typed in some text and the spelling checker has found a mistake, you will need to click on **Cancel** *to close the Spelling dialog box.*

Using the keyboard

This time, try using the keys to select a menu option. In the Menu bar, the **F** in **File** is underlined and can be used together with the **Alt** key to open this menu.

• Press **Alt+F** to open the File menu.

Notice that the **A** in **Save As** is underlined.

• Press **A** to select the **Save As** option.

The Save As dialog box is displayed - again, don't worry just now about what it all means. Notice that the **Cancel** button does not have any letter underlined, so you cannot just press a key to select Cancel. You need to use the **Tab** key so that the **Cancel** button has a dotted line around the word Cancel - the button will also have a thicker black frame when it is active.

- Press the **Tab** key 6 times until the **Cancel** button is active - if you miss it, keep pressing **Tab** until it is active again.

- Press **Enter** to select the active option (**Cancel**).

The dialog box is closed and you are returned to the main document window again.

Experiment

Try experimenting now, use the mouse or keyboard to select an option and then click **Cancel** to cancel it.

- Select **Tools, Word Count**, then click **Close**.

- Select **Edit, Find**, then click **Cancel**.

- Select **File, Page Setup**, then click **Cancel**.

The short cut menu

Another way of selecting certain options is to use the special short cut menu by clicking the right-hand mouse button. A list of useful menu options is then displayed.

- Move the mouse pointer to the main document window and click the right-hand mouse button.

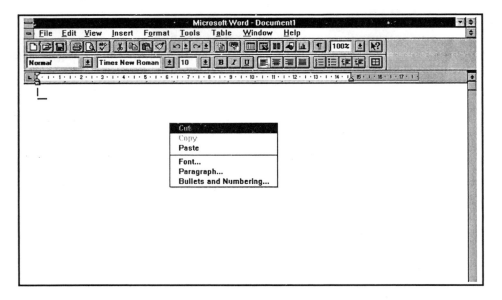

A short cut menu is displayed, showing some options relating to formatting text. Any of the available options can be selected now by clicking on them in the short cut menu.

- Click the right-hand mouse button again to remove the short cut menu.

- Now move the mouse pointer over the toolbar and click the right-hand mouse button.

A different short cut menu is displayed. Generally, the short cut menu will offer options relevant to where the mouse pointer is positioned. It can be a useful way of speeding up certain actions.

- Click the right-hand mouse button again to remove the short cut menu.

Exiting Word

You have now finished your short introduction to the Word environment and it is time to exit Word.

- Open the File menu by clicking on **File** in the menu bar, or by pressing **Alt+F**.

Notice that the x in **Exit** is underlined.

- Select the **Exit** option by clicking on it, or by pressing **X**.

☞ *If you have inadvertently typed anything before selecting **Exit**, Word will think you have started creating a document. As a safety feature, it will ask you if you wish to save the document before it is closed. If this happens, the Save As dialog box is opened and you should click **Cancel** to avoid saving the document.*

☞ *If you are an experienced Windows user, you will also know that you can close any program, Word included, by doubleclicking its Control menu box in the top left-hand corner of the program window.*

- If you are at all uncertain about how to start Word, or how to make menu selections, you should repeat this chapter now.

Your First Document

In this chapter you will create your first document, save it, make a couple of changes and then print it. If you do not have a printer, then you will, of course, not be able to print your document.

- Start your Word program.

- If the Tip of the Day dialog box is displayed, read the tip and then click **OK**.

You should now have an empty document window.

Typing in text

You can now start to type - first a heading, then some text.

- Type:

  What is a computer?

- Press the **Enter** key to conclude the heading.

- Press the **Enter** key again to create an empty line after the heading.

Word wrap

Unlike an ordinary typewriter, there is no need for you to press the carriage return, or **Enter** key, at the end of every line of text. The program takes care of this for you once the cursor reaches the right hand margin. This feature is known as *word wrap*.

☞ *When typing in this and subsequent texts, if you make a mistake then you can use the* **Backspace** *key to delete the mistake, and then re-type the correct text.*

☞ *When typing in this and subsequent texts, the line breaks shown in the course will not necessarily match the line breaks shown on your screen. Do not worry about this, let the program take care of the line breaks with its word wrap feature.*

- Type:

  In simple terms, a computer is no more than an electrical appliance. Like your television, or freezer, it has been developed to be able to perform certain tasks. For example, you can use your computer as a typewriter for writing letters, or as a pocket calculator to do your sums. You can also use it to store telephone numbers, play games, produce technical drawings and develop camera-ready documents for printing. Computers can even be used to run production lines.

- Press the **Enter** key to conclude the paragraph.

- Press the **Enter** key again to create an empty line.

- Type:

  Just like any other electrical appliance, computers can and do break down and cause problems. However, be very sceptical when a mistake is blamed "on the computer". In most cases it's a human error that causes you to receive that notice from British Telecom that says that unless you pay your outstanding bill for £4,567,333, your telephone will be disconnected.

- Press the **Enter** key to conclude the paragraph.

- Press the **Enter** key again to create an empty line.

- Type:

  A computer is not some sort of supernatural, super-intelligent, all-mighty machine, poised to take over the world. A computer can not think for itself, it can only follow instructions. It is not capable of suddenly deciding that it would like to have an ice-cream cone, or of feeling the desire to take a long vacation on some sunny island beach. A computer can, however, follow instructions and perform pre-defined tasks at an amazingly high rate: a million or so instructions per second.

- Press the **Enter** key to conclude the paragraph.

Your screen should now resemble the next picture.

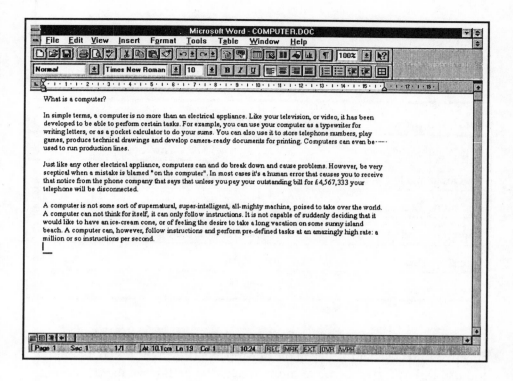

Cursor movement

⊕ The cursor can be moved by means of the arrow keys (**ArrowUp** ↑, **ArrowDown** ↓, **ArrowLeft** ←, **ArrowRight** →) immediately to the right of the main keypad. By pressing one of the arrow keys once, the cursor moves one step in the direction of the arrow.

⊕ Alternatively, the mouse can be used to reposition the cursor any-where in your text. Simply move the mouse pointer controlled by the mouse to the desired position in the text and click the left hand button. The cursor, or insertion point, moves to that position.

Whether you use the arrow keys or the mouse will depend entirely on your own working habits and what you are used to. Many experienced typists prefer to have their fingers close to the "home keys" and therefore use keys rather than the mouse.

☞ *The home keys are **asdf jkl;** used by typists as a reference point for positioning their fingers.*

To rapidly move the cursor to different positions in the text the **Home, End, Page Up, Page Down** and **Arrow** keys are used as described in the following table.

To move the cursor...	*Use the key(s)*
Left/Right one character	**ArrowLeft/ArrowRight**
Up/Down one line at a time	**ArrowUp/ArrowDown**
Beginning/End of line	**Home/End**
Beginning/End of document	**Ctrl+Home/Ctrl+End**
One screen up	**PgUp**
One screen down	**PgDn**

There are a few more key combinations than these. In the beginning, you may just find it easier to click at the desired location in the text if it is shown, and use **PgUp/PgDn** to move more quickly up and down the document.

☞ *In the above table and throughout the course, keys joined together by a + mean that both keys should be pressed at once.*

☞ *When moving the cursor downwards, you cannot position it past the end of document marker (__). Thus, as your screen stands now, assuming you have not altered the text, you will not be able to move the cursor further down than one line after the last paragraph, even though the document window is partially empty.*

• Try using the key combinations now.

Erasing/Deleting text

Two keys can be used to erase/delete text.

 The **Backspace** key is usually located above the **Enter** key on the main keyboard (the alphanumeric section). Pressing this key erases the character immediately to the **left of the cursor**.

 The **Delete** keys (often 2 of them) are usually located on the numeric keypad (**Del**) and in the group of keys above the arrow keys. Pressing the **Delete** key removes the character immediately to the **right of the cursor**.

Deleting characters

In order to change <u>freezer</u> to <u>video</u> using the **Backspace** key:

* With the help of the arrow keys or the mouse, place the cursor immediately after the word <u>freezer</u> in the second sentence.

* Press the **Backspace** key 7 times.

* Type:

  video

Now change <u>British Telecom</u> (towards the end of the first paragraph) to <u>the phone company</u> using the **Delete** key:

* Place the cursor immediately before the <u>B</u> of <u>British Telecom</u>.

* Press the **Delete** key 15 times.

* Type:

  the phone company

You see, it's easy when you know how!

Saving your document

In order to save the text that you have written, you must give your new document a name. Let's call it COMPUTER.DOC.

 The rule for filenames is; up to eight characters for the name and three characters for the extension, separated by a full stop. By default, Word will give your word processing files the extension .DOC, so you only need to type the first part of the filename.

- Insert the exercise diskette provided in drive A.

- Open the **File** menu and select **Save**, or
  click the **Save** button on the toolbar, or
  just press **Ctrl+S**.

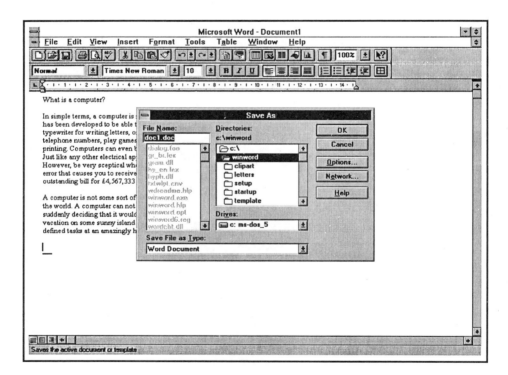

The Save As dialog box is opened allowing you to choose a drive, a directory, a filename and the type of file you wish to save. However, when you are using a diskette, it is quicker to avoid choosing most of the information by typing the drive and filename directly in the File Name box.

Notice also that the entry <u>doc1.doc</u> in the File Name box is highlighted. This means that anything you type now will replace that entry.

- Type:

  a:computer

- Press the **Enter** key (or click **OK**).

☞ *Typing* **a:** *at the beginning of the filename instructs Word to save the document on the exercise disk in drive A - the letter A can be in upper or lower case, but a colon must be entered after it.*

The name of the document is now shown in the document title bar as <u>COMPUTER.DOC</u>.

Printing out

It will now be interesting to see what your document looks like on paper.

- Make sure that your printer is switched on and is "ON LINE", i.e., ready to use.

- Open the **File** menu and select **Print**, or just press **Ctrl+P**.

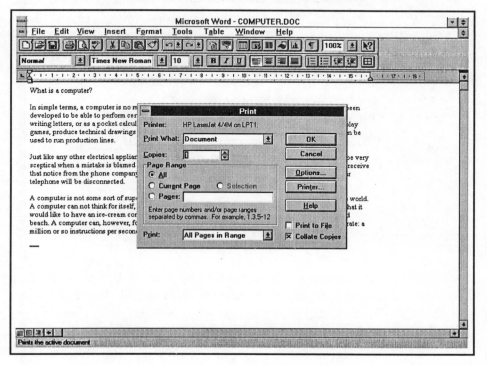

The Print dialog box is opened. As you can see, the default settings are to print 1 copy and All the pages. For now just accept the default settings and try printing out.

- Click on **OK** (or just press **Enter**).

If everything is connected correctly, you should now be the proud possessor of a fine document!

Using the Print button on the toolbar

If you know that the settings in the Print dialog box are as you want them, you can start a printout by simply clicking the **Print** button (pictured left) in the toolbar. The Print dialog box is not opened, but its settings are used to print the document.

Final exercise

- As a final exercise, change <u>video</u> back to <u>freezer</u> and <u>the phone company</u> back to <u>British Telecom</u>.

Save the document again

When the time comes for you to conclude your session with the program you should always finish off by saving your document. As an added precaution Word will warn you if you try to exit without saving whenever you have made any changes since the last time the document was saved.

- Open the **File** menu and select the **Save** option, or
click the **Save** button in the toolbar, or
just press **Ctrl+S**.

The document is automatically saved keeping the same filename, i.e. A:COMPUTER.DOC. Note that this time the Save dialog box is not opened.

Exiting Word

Finally it's time to exit Word again.

- Open the **File** menu.

You have two choices:

⊛ Selecting **Close** will close the current document, but leave Word running.

⊛ Selecting **Exit** will exit Word, closing the current document automatically at the same time.

- Select **Exit** to exit Word.

Your Second Document

In this chapter you will create a second document and save it. You will also use the Print Preview feature to preview the document without printing it out.

- Start your Word program.

- If the Tip of the Day dialog box is displayed, read the tip and then click **OK**.

You should now have an empty document window.

Typing in text

You can now start to type - first a heading, then some text.

- Type:

   What is a modem?

- Press the **Enter** key to conclude the heading.

- Press the **Enter** key again to create an empty line after the heading.

☞ *Remember you can use the* **Backspace** *key if you make a mistake typing.*

☞ *Remember to let Word take care of the line breaks with its word wrap feature.*

- Type:

   Modem is short for Modulator/demodulator. None the wiser? Well, a telephone line is best suited for a human voice and not for transmission of the sort of data your computer likes to send. A modem, which is connected between your computer and the telephone line, converts (modulates) the computer's data signals to more human-like tone signals, which can then be transmitted over the line. Another modem at the other end will receive the call and re-convert (demodulate) it to data signals which the receiving computer can understand.

- Press the **Enter** key to conclude the paragraph.

- Press the **Enter** key again to create an empty line.

- Type:

  A modem can either be a stand-alone unit connected to your computer's serial port and to a telephone line, or an add-in card which is mounted inside the computer.

- Press the **Enter** key to conclude the paragraph.

- Press the **Enter** key again to create an empty line.

- Type:

  The most important feature for a modem is it's transmission speed. This is measured in Baud or bps (bits per second). A higher Baud rate means a faster transmission and a lower telephone bill, but it also means a more expensive modem. It will be a question of measuring up your needs against your means.

- Press the **Enter** key to conclude the paragraph.

Your screen should now resemble the next picture.

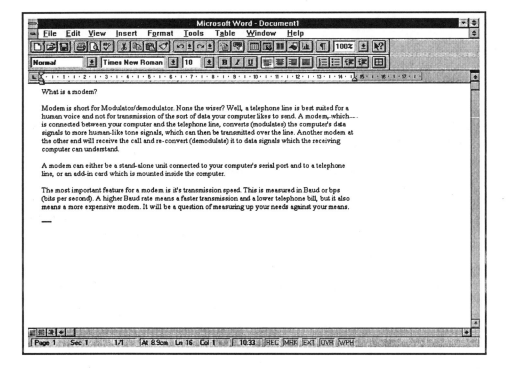

Saving your document

In order to save the text that you have written, you must give your new document a name. Let's call it MODEM.DOC.

- Insert the exercise diskette provided in drive A.

- Open the **File** menu and select **Save**, or
  click the **Save** button on the toolbar, or
  just press **Ctrl+S**.

The Save As dialog box is opened.

- In the File Name box, type:

  a:modem

- Press the **Enter** key (or click **OK**).

☞ *Remember, typing* **a:** *at the beginning of the filename instructs Word to save the document on drive A.*

The name of the document is now shown in the document title bar as <u>MODEM.DOC</u>.

Print Preview

Instead of printing out the document, you can use Print Preview to view the document on screen. Print Preview will show you exactly what the document will look like when it is printed.

- Open the **File** menu and select **Print Preview**, or
  click the **Print Preview** button on the toolbar.

The Print Preview window is opened (see picture on next page) showing you a whole page view of your document. Notice that the mouse pointer now looks like a magnifying glass.

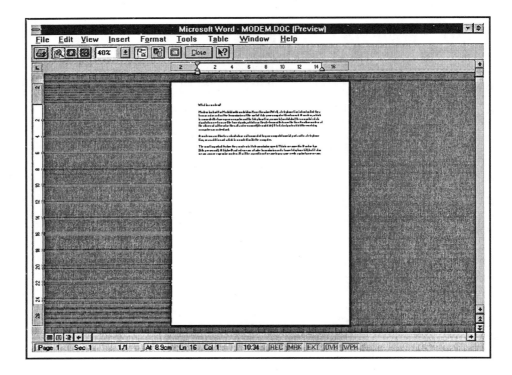

- Move the mouse pointer and click on some text in the document.

The text is magnified.

- Click on the text in the document again.

The document is reduced again.

Now close the Print Preview window:

- Click the **Close** button in the toolbar.

The document window is displayed again.

Adding more text

Now add some more text. Start off by moving the cursor down to the end of the document:

- Press **Ctrl+End**.

- Press **Enter** to create an empty line.

- Type the following text, adding empty lines as necessary:

Serial port

A serial port is a special sort of connector through which your computer can send data to the outside world, which might happen to be for example a modem or a serial printer.

If you have an external modem, i.e. stand-alone modem, then it will also have a serial port which has to be connected to a serial port on your computer.

Most computers have one, or two, serial ports, but it is possible that you will need to buy an extra serial port if, for example, you are using the present one(s) for a serial mouse and/or a serial printer, or some other computer add-on.

Ending the session

Finally it's time to exit Word again.

- Open the **File** menu and select **Exit**.

You did not save the document before trying to exit Word, so Word now asks you if you want to save the changes you made.

- Make sure your exercise diskette is in drive A.

- Click **Yes**.

Word saves the document for you and then exits.

Open, Close, New, Save As

In this chapter, you will practise opening and closing documents and also learn how to open a new document. When opening a document, you can either type in the drive and filename, or use the Drives and Directories boxes to search for a document. Both methods are covered. Using **Save As** to save a document with a different filename, and opening a document with a different format are also covered.

- Start Word.

- If the Tip of the Day dialog box is displayed, read the tip and then click **OK**.

You should now have an empty document window.

Opening and closing a document

So far in this course you have created and saved two documents on your exercise diskette; COMPUTER.DOC and MODEM.DOC. As long as these documents are not deleted, they can be opened at any time.

You will now open COMPUTER.DOC by typing in the drive name and filename, just as you did when you saved it.

- Make sure your exercise diskette is in drive A.

- Select **File**, **Open**, or
click the **Open** button on the toolbar, or
just press **Ctrl+O**.

The Open dialog box is displayed.

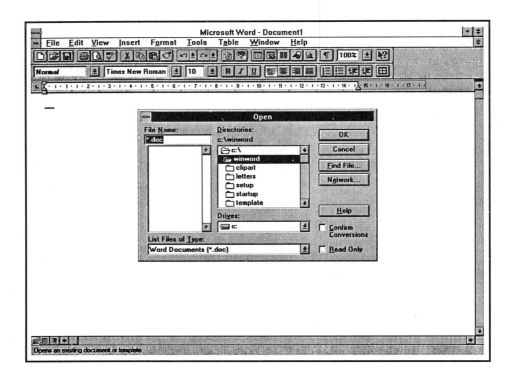

A list of available documents in the current directory is shown. Note that the cursor is flashing in the File Name box, and that the current entry is highlighted. This means that you can simply type the drive and filename of the desired document and it will replace the current entry.

- Type:

  a:computer

- Click **OK**, or press **Enter**.

The document is opened for you and you could work on it, although just now you will close it again.

- Select **File, Close**, to close the document again.

☝ *Remember that closing a document does not exit Word altogether.*

Open - using the Drives box

This time, you will open a document using the Drives box, and then looking for the document filename in the list of files available. Try opening the MODEM.DOC document as follows:

- Make sure your exercise diskette is in drive A.

- Select **File**, **Open**, or
  click the **Open** button on the toolbar, or
  just press **Ctrl+O**.

The Open dialog box is displayed and a list of available documents in the current directory is shown.

- Click anywhere on the Drives box to open a list of available drives.

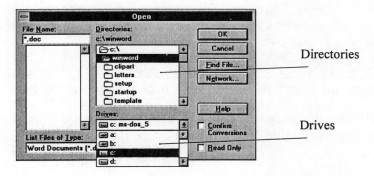

- Click the **a:** drive option in the list.

After a short pause, the list of files is updated to show the available files in drive A.

- In the list of files, look for the file MODEM.DOC.

☞ *If the file you are looking for is not visible, you can scroll the list using the vertical scroll bar. You can also click on any filename in the list and then use the* **ArrowDown** *key to move down the list of files.*

- Doubleclick the filename MODEM.DOC, or select the filename and then click **OK**.

Your MODEM.DOC document is opened.

Clearing the screen

Assume that you wish to clear the current text from the screen in order to start a new document.

New or Close?

At this stage it is important to clarify the difference between the **New** and **Close** options in the **File** menu.

If you select **New**, the screen will be apparently cleared, but in effect a new empty document window will be opened *on top of* the current document. This is because Word for Windows allows you to work with several documents open at any time.

If you select **Close**, the current document window is closed and removed completely from the screen. Presuming there aren't any other documents open, you will be left without a document window. You can then select **New** to open a fresh document window.

Thus, if as a rule you only work with a single document at a time, to clear the screen you should select the **Close** option and then open a **New** document.

☞ *A quicker way of closing a document is to doubleclick the Control menu box for the document window, but don't mix it up with the Control menu box for the Word program itself, which would exit the program.*

☞ *Remember, anytime you try to close a document that has been changed since it was last saved, you will be asked if you wish to save the changes.*

• Select **File, Close**.

The current document window containing MODEM.DOC is closed.

Opening a new document

You will now open a new document, but using the **New** button and using the menu option have slightly different results.

Using File, New

* Select **File, New**.

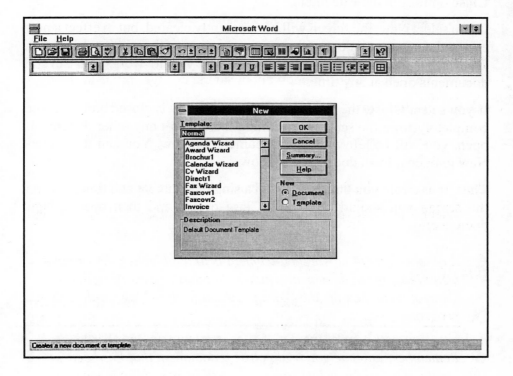

Each time you open a new document in this manner, you will be asked which template you wish to attach to the new document. Templates are covered in a later chapter, and for now you can accept the **Normal** option.

* Click **OK**.

A new document is opened for you.

Using the New button or Ctrl+N

 If you use the **New** button on the toolbar, or the short cut key combination **Ctrl+N**, you do not have to go through the process of selecting a template.

- Click the **New** button on the toolbar, or just press **Ctrl+N.**

A second new document is opened for you and you can begin typing.

- Type:
  This text is just a test sentence and will not be saved.

Closing without saving

You will now close a document without saving changes made to it.

- Select **File, Close**.

A dialog box is opened asking you if you want to save the changes.

- Click **No**.

The first new document is now visible again and you can close this too.

- Select **File, Close**, if you are asked about saving the changes, select **No** again.

Browsing

If you can't remember what a document was called, or where it was saved, you can use the Drives and Directories boxes to look for the file. In this example, you will inspect the .DOC files available on your hard disk, but not open any of them.

- Select **File, Open**, or
  click the **Open** button on the toolbar, or
  just press **Ctrl+O**.

The Open dialog box is displayed and a list of available documents in the current directory is shown.

Changing the drive

- Click anywhere on the Drives box to open a list of available drives.

- Click the **c:** drive option in the list.

The list of available files is updated - it may be empty!

Changing the directory

You can also change the directory to search in different directories.

- In the Directories list, doubleclick the **c:** option at the top of the list.

The list of files now shows .DOC files in the root directory of your hard disk - the list may be empty!

- In the Directories list, locate and doubleclick the **dos** directory.

The list of available files is updated - probably empty!

- Locate and doubleclick the **c:** option at the top of the Directories list again.

- Locate and doubleclick the **winword** directory in the Directories list.

This time, you can see in the Directories list that the **winword** directory has several subdirectories which could also be selected.

- Locate and doubleclick the **c:** option at the top of the Directories list again.

- Locate and doubleclick the **wordcbt** directory in the Directories list.

List Files of Type

So far you have been looking for .DOC files, but you can change this.

- Click anywhere on the List Files of Type box, to open the list.

See picture on next page...

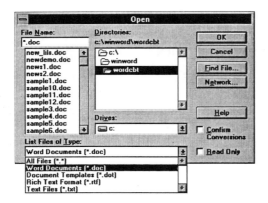

- Click the **All files (*.*)** option.

The list of available files is updated to show all files in the current directory.

Changing the file mask

Another option is to decide yourself which files to look for. You could choose to list all files beginning with M, or all files whose extension starts with P, for example.

- Open the Drives box and select drive **a:**.

- Doubleclick on the entry in the File Name box, so that the whole of the entry is highlighted.

- Type:

  m*.*

- Press **Enter**.

The list of available files is updated again. Try another:

- Doubleclick on the entry in the File Name box, so that the whole of the entry is highlighted again.

- Type:

  .p

- Press **Enter**.

The list of available files is updated once again.

Finish off by restoring the file type to Word Documents again:

- Click anywhere on the List Files of Type box, to open the list.

- Click the **Word Documents (*.doc)** option.

Cancelling the Open dialog box

Assume now that you could not find the file you wanted and want to close the Open dialog box.

- Click **Cancel** to close the Open dialog box.

Save As

When you want to save a document, there are two choices in the **File** menu, **Save** and **Save As**. It is worth remembering the following points:

☺ When you save a document for the first time, i.e. it doesn't already have a filename, the Save As dialogue box is opened regardless of whether you select the **Save** or **Save As** option. You can then give the document a filename.

☺ If your document already has a filename and you wish to save it again with the same name, you should select **File**, **Save** (or use the **Save** button, or press **Ctrl+S**). No dialog box is opened and your document is saved automatically. You can then close it or carry on working with it.

- If your document already has a filename, but you wish to save it with a different filename, then select **File**, **Save As**. The Save As dialog box is opened and you can give the document its new file-name. You can then close it or carry on working.

Try it out now by opening the COMPUTER.DOC file and then saving it on your exercise diskette with a new name COMP2.DOC.

- Make sure your exercise diskette is in drive A.

- Select **File**, **Open**, or
  click the **Open** button on the toolbar, or
  just press **Ctrl+O**.

The Open dialog box is displayed.

- Locate and doubleclick the filename COMPUTER.DOC in the list of files.

The document is opened for you. Now save it with a different name:

- Select **File, Save As**.

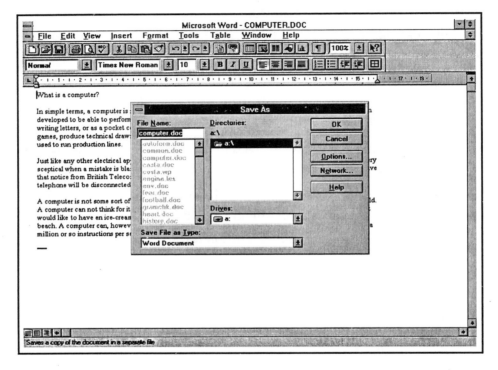

The Save As dialog box is opened.

- In the File Name box, type:

  a:comp2

- Click **OK** (or press **Enter**).

The old COMPUTER.DOC window has been renamed, and you are left with the new COMP2.DOC window instead. You can continue working with the new document, or close it.

- Select **File, Close**.

Opening and saving documents not created in Word for Windows

Assume that somebody just gave you a file from WordPerfect that you need to work on and save in Word format. Such a file, COSTA.WP is on your exercise diskette and you will now open it using many of the features you have just learnt.

- Make sure your exercise diskette is in drive A.

- Select **File**, **Open**, or
  click the **Open** button on the toolbar, or
  just press **Ctrl+O**.

- Drive A should already be selected in the Drives box, if not select the **a:** drive option in the Drives list.

The list of files is updated to show the available *.DOC files in drive A. However, your file is not a .DOC file, you know it has a .WP extension.

- Doubleclick on the entry in the File Name box, so that the whole of the entry is highlighted.

- Type:

  *.wp

- Press **Enter**.

The list of available files is updated again and the one .WP file is in the list.

- Doubleclick the COSTA.WP file in the list.

Although it is a WordPerfect file, Word quickly converts it and opens the document for you.

Saving the document in Word format

The final stage is to use **Save As** to save the document with a new filename MYCOSTA.DOC, in Word format.

- Select **File**, **Save As**.

- In the File Name box, type:

  a:mycosta

- Click anywhere on the Save File as Type box, to open the list.

- Locate and click the **Word Document** option.

- Click **OK**.

Your document is saved in Word format.

- Select **File, Close**.

Recently opened files

☞ *A list of the most recently opened files is shown at the bottom of the File menu allowing you to quickly select and open them.*

- Open the **File** menu, and click one of the files at the bottom of the list.

The file is opened for you.

- Select **File, Close**.

Ending the session

- Select **File, Exit**, to exit Word.

Views, Toolbars and Other Options

There are a number of options available that will enable you to customise Word for Windows, adapting it to your own personal tastes and requirements. Most of these options are available through the **Tools**, **Options** menu. It is also possible to hide or show different toolbars and the Ruler. This is done via the **View** menu.

The different views

Word has different views, each of which can be accessed via the **View** menu. Some of the views also have a button in the Status bar in the bottom left-hand corner of the display. The different views are discussed below.

- The **Normal** view shows a simplified version of your document and is the best all round view for entering, editing and formatting your document.

- The **Outline** view allows you to collapse a document to see only the main headings and expand it to see all the document again. This is particularly useful for scrolling through long documents.

- The **Page Layout** view displays your document as it will be printed, but will slow down your work if you use it for general typing and editing.

- The **Full Screen** view allows you to clear the screen and show just the document itself.

- **Print Preview** shows an entire page at a reduced size. You can also display multiple pages at the same time. This is useful to see the 'balance' of a document spread over several pages.

- The **Zoom** feature allows you to zoom in or zoom out on your document.

- Open the file COMMUN.DOC from your exercise diskette.

- Select **View**, **Page Layout**, or click the **Page Layout View** button.

The document is now shown as it will be printed.

- Select **View**, **Full Screen**.

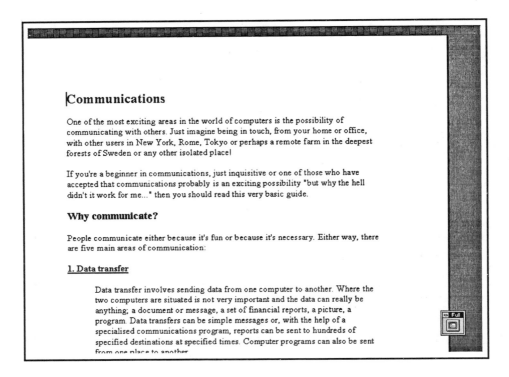

The screen is cleared of all but the document itself, and it is still in the Page Layout view. You can work on the document in this view. There may be a **Full Screen** button displayed somewhere on the screen.

- Click the **Full Screen** button, or press **Esc** to close the Full View.

- Select **View**, **Normal**, or click the **Normal View** button.

The document is now shown in the Normal view again.

- Click on the **Zoom Control** arrow and select **Page Width**.

The document is now enlarged so that it fits the width of the display.

- Click on the **Zoom Control** arrow and select **75%**.

The document is now reduced showing more of it at once.

- Click on the **Zoom Control** arrow and select **100%**.

The document is now restored to its original display size.

Toolbars

You have already used the buttons in the toolbar. The Standard toolbar is the one normally displayed, but Word has several different toolbars. Each toolbar relates to a set of tasks such as formatting, borders, etc. There is also a Word for Windows 2 toolbar which resembles the earlier version of the program.

You can choose exactly which toolbars you want to display.

- Open the **View** menu and select **Toolbars**.

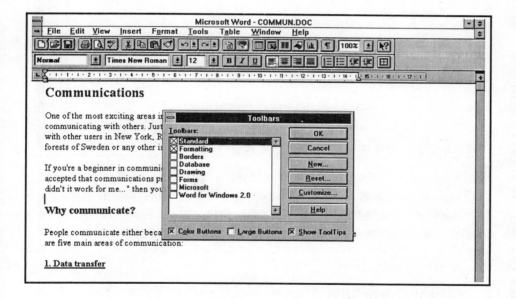

- Click the **Borders** and **Drawing** options so that they are crossed.

- Click **OK**.

The two new toolbars are added to the display. Note that the Drawing toolbar is at the foot of the display.

- Open the **View** menu and select **Toolbars**.

- Click the **Standard, Formatting, Borders** and **Drawing** options so that they are NOT crossed.

- Click **OK**.

All the toolbars are now hidden.

- Open the **View** menu and select **Toolbars**.

- Click the **Standard** and **Formatting** options so that they are crossed.

- Click **OK**.

The Standard and Formatting toolbars are displayed again.

Hiding and showing the Ruler

The Ruler can also be hidden or displayed.

- Select the **View, Ruler** option.

The Ruler is now hidden (or shown if it was hidden before).

- Select the **View, Ruler** option.

The Ruler is now displayed again (or hidden).

Showing non-printing characters

When you type in text, only the text itself is displayed. Certain characters, like end of paragraph markers, spaces, tabs, etc., are not shown. Such characters are often referred to as *non-printing* characters. It may be very useful to display these characters in the document. For example, it is very useful to see where tabs have been inserted, or where a double space has been inserted by mistake.

 - Click the **Show/Hide P** button (pictured left).

The non-printing characters are now displayed.

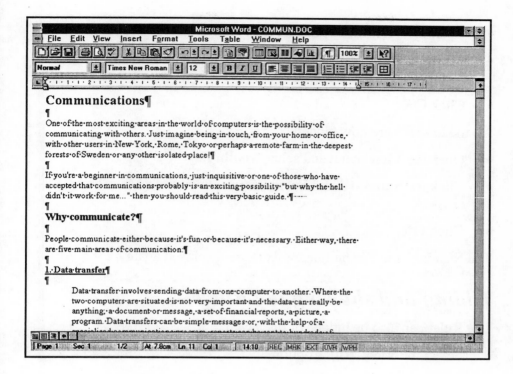

- Click the **Show/Hide P** button again.

The non-printing characters are hidden again.

Options for customising Word

Word has an extensive set of options that will allow you to customise your program. The options themselves are not covered in this course, but as you progress you may want to start making changes. To inspect the different options, proceed as follows:

- Select **Tools, Options**.

Twelve different card files are presented, each has its own set of options.

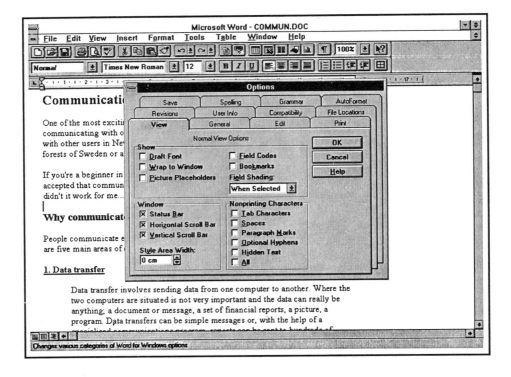

- Click on any of the card tabs to view the options available.

When you are ready, close the Options dialog box:

- Click **Cancel**.

The **Tools, Customize** option also allows you to edit the toolbars, the menu itself and some keyboard items. None of this is covered in this course, and you should be very confident before attempting any changes yourself.

Changing the units of measurement

One option that you may want to change is the units of measurement. You can choose to display measurements in inches, centimetres, points or picas This is done via the **Tools, General** option.

- Select **Tools, Options**.

- Click the **General** tab.

At the foot of the dialog box, there is a Measurement Units option.

• Open the Measurement Units list.

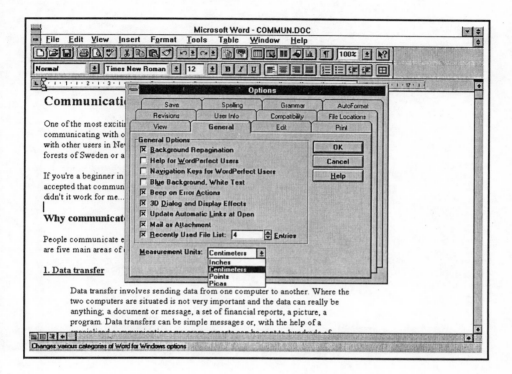

• Select the units of your choice.

☞ *For your convenience, this course will display all measurements in both inches and centimetres.*

• Click **OK** to confirm the change or **Cancel** to close the dialog box without keeping any change you have made.

Ending the session

• Close the current document, do not save any changes.

• Exit Word.

Selecting Text for Editing

Whenever you want to change the style of a particular piece of text - for instance to put it into italics or bold - you should first select the block of text you want to alter and then select the desired feature. Selecting blocks of text allows you to format letters, words, groups of words, sentences or paragraphs all in one go.

Selecting text

You can select any continuous section of text. There are also a few short-cuts for selecting complete words, sentences, paragraphs or the whole document. Any section of text will remain selected until you use one of the cursor position keys (e.g. an **Arrow** key or **PgUp**) or click the mouse anywhere in the document window.

It is possible to use the keyboard or the mouse to select blocks of text - both methods are covered in this chapter. Which method you use will be a matter of personal preference, but being able to use both methods has its advantages.

Start off by opening the document FEAR.DOC from your exercise diskette.

- Start your Word program.

- If the Tip of the Day dialog box is displayed, read the tip and then click **OK**.

- Make sure your exercise diskette is in drive A.

- Select **File**, **Open**, or
click the **Open** button on the toolbar, or
just press **Ctrl+O**.

The Open dialog box is displayed.

- In the File Name box, type:
a:fear

- Click **OK** (or press **Enter**).

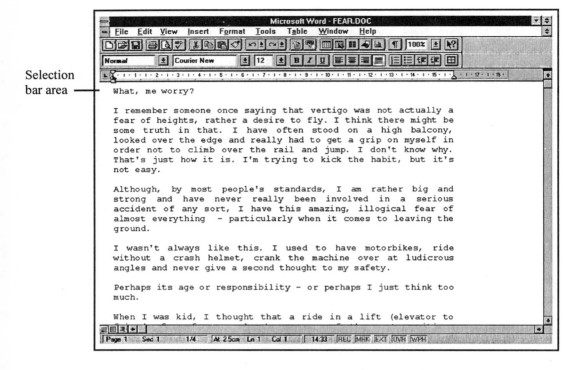

Selection bar area

Using the mouse

First of all, concentrate on using the mouse to select text. The selection bar, which is the area to the left of the text as shown in the picture above, is used to select some units of text.

When you move the mouse pointer over the selection bar, the cursor changes to an arrow, pointing diagonally up to the right.

Selecting a phrase

To use the mouse to select a phrase, simply drag the mouse over the text you want to select. Try selecting the phrase <u>desire to fly</u>.

• Position the mouse pointer just before the letter <u>d</u> in <u>desire</u>.

• Press and hold down the left mouse button.

• Drag the mouse to the right until the phrase <u>desire to fly</u> is selected, then release the mouse button.

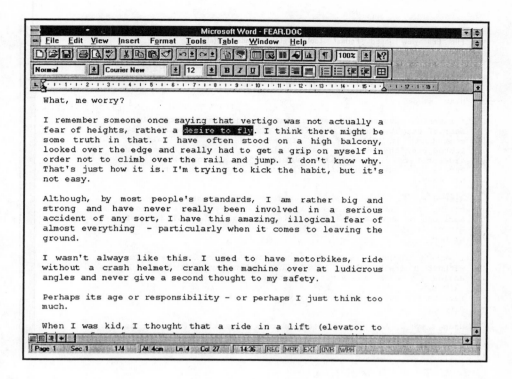

☞ *If you extend your selection too far, you can reverse the end of the selecting by pressing* **Shift+ArrowLeft**.

☞ *If the section you want to select extends beyond the bottom of the screen, simply move the mouse pointer, keeping the button depressed, below the bottom border to scroll the text.*

• Click anywhere on the document to remove the selection highlight.

Selecting a single word

You can also select individual words by doubleclicking them.

• Point to somewhere in the word <u>vertigo</u>.

• Doubleclick on the word.

The whole word is selected.

• Click anywhere on the document to remove the selection highlight.

Selecting a sentence

A sentence can be selected by using the **Ctrl** key together with the mouse.
Try selecting any sentence as follows:

- Hold down the **Ctrl** key and click anywhere in the desired sentence.

The sentence is selected.

- Click anywhere on the document to remove the selection highlight.

Selecting a line of text

To select a complete line of text using the mouse, you need to point to the
selection bar, i.e. on the left edge of the text.

- Point to the selection bar to the left of any line of text and click the
  mouse.

The chosen line of text is selected.

- Click anywhere on the document to remove the selection highlight.

Selecting a paragraph

There are two ways of selecting a paragraph with the mouse:

- Tripleclick anywhere on the paragraph
- Point to the selection bar to the left of the paragraph and doubleclick the mouse.

- Tripleclick anywhere on the third paragraph.

The paragraph is selected.

- Click anywhere on the document to remove the selection highlight.

Selecting a whole document

To select the whole document, tripleclick on the selection bar.

- Point to the selection bar and then tripleclick the mouse.

The whole text is selected.

- Click anywhere on the document to remove the selection highlight.

Using the keyboard

Now try using the keyboard to select some text.

Selecting a phrase

To select a phrase, first move the cursor to one end of the text you want to select. Try selecting the phrase not actually a fear.

• Move the cursor just before the n in not in the first paragraph.

• Press **Shift+ArrowRight**.

Note how the n is selected. Each time you use **Shift+ArrowKey**, then the selection will be extended one character/line in the direction of the arrow.

• Press **Shift+ArrowRight** again.

Note how the selection is extended.

• Press **Shift+ArrowRight** a further seventeen times.

You should now have selected the phrase not actually a fear.

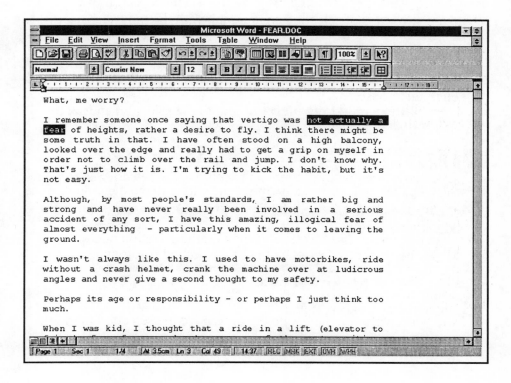

☝ *If you extend your selecting too far, you can reverse the end of the selection by using* **Shift+ArrowLeft**.

Selecting a single word

Selecting a word at a time is done with the help of the key combination **Shift+Ctrl**.

- Move the cursor just before the word <u>vertigo</u>.

- Press **Shift+Ctrl+ArrowRight**.

The whole word is selected.

You can skip forward selecting the following words by pressing **Shift+Ctrl+ArrowRight** again, or skip backwards using **Shift+Ctrl+ArrowLeft**.

Selecting a sentence

To select a sentence, you should use the same method as selecting a word. If the sentence is longer than a line of text, you can quickly select the line using **Shift+End**. Try selecting the very first sentence as follows.

- Move the cursor to the beginning of the first sentence (not the title).

- Press **Shift+End** to select the line.

- Press **Shift+ArrowDown** to extend the selecting downwards.

- Press **Shift+ArrowLeft** a few times until the selection ends at the end of the sentence.

Selecting a paragraph

To select a paragraph, you need to move the cursor to the beginning of the paragraph, and then press **Shift+Ctrl+ArrowDown**. Try selecting the second paragraph now.

- Move the cursor to the beginning of the second paragraph.

- Press **Shift+Ctrl+ArrowDown**.

The whole paragraph is selected.

Selecting a whole document

To select the whole document, use **Ctrl+A**.

- Press **Ctrl+A**.

The whole text is selected.

Extending a selected text

Any selected text can be extended, or shortened, a character or line at a time using **Shift+Arrow** key. Using **Ctrl+Shift+Arrow** key will extend the selection a word or paragraph at a time. This applies even if the original selection was done with the mouse.

- Take some time selecting some text blocks and then extending and shortening them.

Ending the session

Finally, close the current document. If asked, do not save any changes.

- Select **File, Close**.
- Exit Word.

Summary

The following table summarises the available selection procedures.

To select...	*Keyboard*	*Mouse*
Any text block	**Shift+Arrow keys**	LEFT button and drag
One character l/r	**Shift+ArrowRight/Left**	
One line up/ down	**Shift+ArrowUp/Down**	
Word	**Ctrl+Shift+ArrowRight/Left**	Doubleclick on word
Sentence	Combination of line and word, Press **Ctrl** and click anywhere on sentence	Hold down **Ctrl** and click on sentence
Line of text	**Shift+End**	Point on selection bar beside line and click
Paragraph	**Ctrl+Shift+ArrowDown/Up**	Tripleclick on paragraph, or point on selection bar by paragraph and doubleclick
Whole document	**Ctrl+A**	Tripleclick anywhere on the selection bar

Bold, Italics & Underlining

In order to emphasise headings and other important sections of your text, Word offers you several different alternatives such as **bold**, *italics* and underlining. In this chapter, you will learn how to apply these styles to a document.

- Start your Word program.

- If the Tip of the Day dialog box is displayed, read the tip and then click **OK**.

You should have an empty document window.

Applying the features

These features can be applied to existing text, or as you type in new text. There are three ways of selecting each feature:

☺ Use the **Format, Font** menu option.

☺ Use the short cut key combinations **Ctrl+B**, **Ctrl+I** and **Ctrl+U**.

B ☺ Use the buttons (shown left) on the toolbar.

I In the following example, you will apply the features to the document MEMORY.DOC, which you can open now:

U
- Make sure your exercise diskette is in drive A.

- Select **File, Open**, or
  click the **Open** button on the toolbar, or
  just press **Ctrl+O**.

The Open dialog box is displayed.

- In the File Name box, type:

  a:memory

- Click **OK**, or press **Enter**.

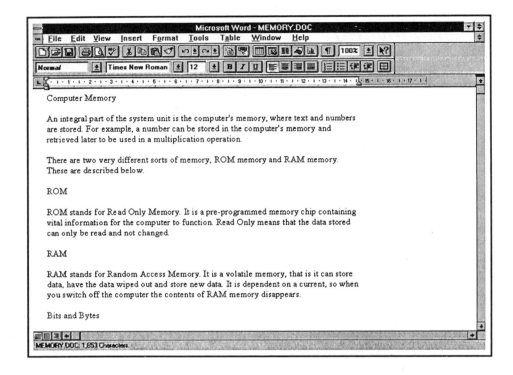

Bold

You make any text in your document bold by selecting the desired text and then applying the bold feature.

- Select the first heading, <u>Computer Memory</u>, by tripleclicking anywhere on it.

- Click the **Bold** button (or press **Ctrl+B**) to apply the bold style.

- Click anywhere on the text to remove the highlight.

The first heading is now displayed as bold text.

- Select the second heading, <u>ROM Memory</u>, by tripleclicking anywhere on it.

- Click the **Bold** button (or press **Ctrl+B**) to apply the bold style.

- Click anywhere on the text to remove the highlight.

- Finally, do the same for the remaining headings <u>RAM Memory</u>, <u>Bits and Bytes</u> and <u>Memory Size</u>.

Underlining text

In the same way as with bold, you can underline text as you type or add underlining to existing text. In this case however, it is the **Underline** button in the toolbar that is used - or the **Ctrl+U** key combination.

- Select the phrase <u>Read Only Memory</u> in the 3rd paragraph.

- Click the **Underline** button (or press **Ctrl+U**), to turn the underline feature ON.

- Click anywhere on the text to remove the highlight.

The phrase is underlined.

- Select the phrase <u>Random Access Memory</u> in the next paragraph.

- Click the **Underline** button (or press **Ctrl+U**), to turn the underline feature ON.

- Click anywhere on the text to remove the highlight.

The phrase is underlined.

Italics

Once again, applying italics is exactly the same as applying the bold or underlined features to your text, except, of course, that you use the **Italics** button in the toolbar, or the short cut key combination **Ctrl+I**.

- Select the phrase <u>1 kilobyte</u> in the 6th paragraph.

- Click the **Italics** button (or press **Ctrl+I**) to turn the italics feature ON.

- Click anywhere on the text to remove the highlight.

Combining features

It is perfectly OK to combine the different feature. For example, you can make a heading bold, italic and underlined, in fact you can add and remove features to any selected text.

Change the first heading to be bold, italic and underlined:

- Select the first heading, <u>Computer Memory</u>, by tripleclicking any-where on it.

- Click the **Italics** button (or press **Ctrl+I**) to apply italics.

Without removing the selection highlight, you can continue to apply different features:

- Click the **Underline** button (or press **Ctrl+U**) to apply underlining.

- Click anywhere on the text to remove the highlight.

Removing a feature

Now remove the italics feature from the main heading:

- Select the first heading, <u>Computer Memory</u>, by tripleclicking any-where on it.

- Click the **Italics** button (or press **Ctrl+I**) to remove the italics.

Click anywhere on the text to remove the highlight. The title is now bold and underlined only.

Using the features as you type

All these features can be applied as you type. Try this:

- Move the cursor down to the end of the document (**Ctrl+End**).

- Press **Enter** to create an empty line.

- Click the **Bold** button, or press **Ctrl+B**, to turn the bold feature ON.

Notice how the **Bold** button has changed, indicating that the bold feature is on.

- Type:

  Good Advice

- Click the **Bold** button, or press **Ctrl+B** again to turn the bold fea-ture OFF.

- Press **Enter** twice to conclude the paragraph and create an empty line.

- Click the **Underline** button (or press **Ctrl+U**), to turn the underline feature ON.

Notice how the **Underline** button has changed, indicating that the underline feature is on.

- Type:

If you use Windows

- Click the **Underline** button (or press **Ctrl+U**) again to turn the underline feature OFF.

- Click the **Italics** button, or press **Ctrl+I**, to turn the italics feature ON.

- Type, starting with a space:

make sure you have plenty of memory!

- Click the **Italics** button, or press **Ctrl+I** again to turn the italics feature OFF.

- Press **Enter** to move down one line.

Print the document

Now print the document to see what you have created.

- Make sure your printer is ready to print.

- Click the **Print** button on the toolbar.

Experiment

- Spend a little time selecting phrases and applying the different features to them.

Ending the session

- Select **File**, **Close**, do not save any changes to the document.

- Select **File**, **Exit**, to exit Word.

Copying and Moving Text

Copying and moving text in Word is a relatively simple process and makes use of Windows' Clipboard which is a *buffer*, or temporary storage space in your computer's memory. The basics of using the Clipboard - cut, copy and paste - are covered in this chapter. You will also learn to copy information between two documents and the art of *drag and drop*.

- Start your Word program.

- If the Tip of the Day dialog box is displayed, read the tip and then click **OK**.

You should have an empty document window and can open the file COSTA.DOC from your exercise diskette.

- Make sure your exercise diskette is in drive A.

- Select **File**, **Open**, or
  click the **Open** button on the toolbar, or
  just press **Ctrl+O**.

The Open dialog box is displayed.

- In the File Name box, type:

  a:costa

- Click **OK**, or press **Enter**.

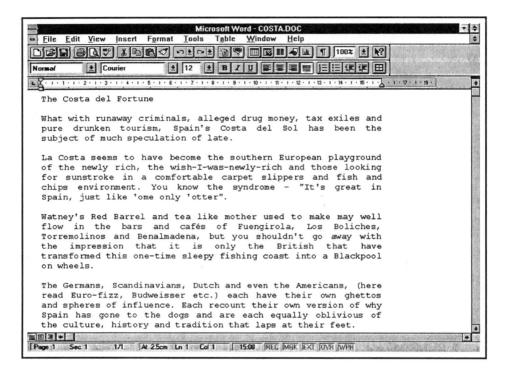

Using Clipboard

Clipboard is a temporary storage place for text, graphics, tables, etc., and can be used to move items around within a document and between different documents. It has three basic operations - Cut, Copy and Paste as described in the table below.

Feature	Key	Description
Cut	**Ctrl+X**	Deletes the selected text (or item) from the document and stores a copy of it in Clipboard.
Copy	**Ctrl+C**	Stores a copy of the selected text (or item) in Clipboard without changing the document.
Paste	**Ctrl+V**	Inserts a copy of what is in Clipboard into the document at the cursor's position.

It is important to note the following:

⊕ Only one block of text can be stored in the Clipboard at a time, and it is always the last block that you either cut or copied that is stored. Thus, if you have one block of text stored in Clipboard, the next time you cut or copy a block of text, the new block will **replace** the old block in Clipboard.

⊕ Clipboard is shared by all other Windows applications, so if you go to another application and perform a cut or copy operation, the current item in the Clipboard will be replaced, wherever it came from.

Short cut buttons

There are three short cut buttons on the toolbar to speed up your work, from left to right, **Cut**, **Copy** and **Paste**.

Cutting text

To perform a cut you select the desired text, then cut it. Cut is used to delete text, or in conjunction with Paste, to move text.

☞ *Remember, using Cut removes the selected text from your document and stores a copy in Clipboard.*

• In the first main paragraph, select the phrase <u>alleged drug money,</u> (including the comma and blank space after it).

• Select **Edit, Cut**, or
click the **Cut** button on the toolbar, or
press **Ctrl+X).**

The text is removed from the document and a copy of the text is automatically stored in Clipboard. As long as it remains in Clipboard, a copy of the text can be inserted, or *pasted*, as many times as you like into your document and at any position. Furthermore, you could even create or open another document and insert a copy of the text into it.

Undoing a cut

It is quite possible that you may cut a block of text in error. If you realise this straight away, before you do anything else, you can **undo** the cut automatically by selecting the **Undo** option from the **Edit** menu (or pressing **Ctrl+Z**).

- Select **Edit**, **Undo Cut**, or press **Ctrl+Z**.

- Click anywhere on the document to remove the selection highlight.

The document is restored to its former state prior to carrying out the cut operation.

Copying text

To copy text (or other item), select the desired text block, then copy it. Copy is often used to duplicate a phrase, sentence or paragraph.

☞ *Remember, using Copy copies the selected text to Clipboard without altering your document.*

- Select the whole of the second paragraph (tripleclick on it).

- Select **Edit**, **Copy**, or
  click the **Copy** button on the toolbar, or
  press **Ctrl+C**.

- Click anywhere on the document to remove the selection highlight.

A copy of the paragraph is now in Clipboard.

Pasting text

To paste text (or other item) from Clipboard, position the cursor where the item is to be pasted and paste it.

Paste inserts a copy of whatever is in Clipboard into your document at the cursor's position. After following the last two instructions, you will have a copy of the second paragraph in Clipboard. The phrase <u>alleged drug money,</u> is no longer there, it was wiped out when the second paragraph was copied as only one item at a time can be stored in Clipboard.

- Move the cursor to the very end of the document (**Ctrl+End**) and press **Enter** twice to create some space.

- Select **Edit, Paste,** or
  click the **Paste** button on the toolbar, or
  press **Ctrl+V**.

A copy of the paragraph is pasted into your document. You could, in fact, paste the same text block many times - as long as nothing else is cut or copied into Clipboard.

Drag and drop

Having learnt the basics of cutting, copying and pasting, it will be useful to learn the drag and drop technique. This is suitable for moving or copying selected text over a short distance in the document. For longer distances, Cut, Copy and Paste are more convenient.

☺ To move text, select the text, then point to the selected text, hold down the mouse button, and drag the dotted insertion point over to the new position. When in position, release the mouse button.

☺ To copy text, do exactly the same as above, but hold down the **Ctrl** key when you drag the dotted insertion point over.

Try it out now:

- Select the phrase Torremolinos and Benalmedena in the 3rd paragraph, including the comma and space after the comma.

- Position the mouse pointer over the middle of the selected text.

- Hold down the left-hand mouse button and drag the small dotted insertion line until it is positioned immediately before the L in Los Boliches.

- Release the mouse button.

- Click anywhere on the document to remove the selection highlight.

The phrase should now have been moved to its new position.

Now move the first paragraph:

- Select the whole of the first paragraph (tripleclick on it).

- Position the mouse pointer over the middle of the selected text.

- Hold down the left-hand mouse button and drag the small dotted insertion line until it is positioned immediately between the second and third paragraphs.

- Release the mouse button.

Exercise

- Experiment on your own, deleting, copying and moving blocks of text, using drag and drop and Cut, Copy and Paste.

- When you are ready, select **File**, **Close**, do not save the changes.

Working with two or more documents

In Word, you can have several documents open at any one time. You can either have the current document on display and the others in effect hidden, or alternatively, you can divide the screen into two or more smaller windows and thereby display more documents on the screen simultaneously.

Start off by opening a new document.

- Click the **New** button on the toolbar or press **Ctrl+N**.

You should now have have a fresh document.

- Type:
  Those Magnificent Men

- Press the **Enter** key twice.

- Type:

  Since the beginning of time man has had the desire, even urge, to fly. History and reference books are generously illustrated with some of man's first attempts. Strange figures boasting home made wings with real feathers glued to their surfaces and wonderful Heath Robinson-style contraptions apparently held together with string and tape, with flapping ineffective wings and little chance of ever leaving the ground. Even one of history's most inventive and creative thinkers - Leonardo da Vinci - sketched and built 15th century models of flying machines and recognisable helicopter prototypes. However, it was not until the 20th century that man managed to realise his dream and finally leave the ground in powered flight.

- Press the **Enter** key twice.

- Type:

  As we approach the 21st century with supersonic air travel and space flight so much of a reality, that we hardly turn our heads when the latest space shuttle or TV satellite is launched, it is hard to imagine that some people can still remember when air travel was an unfulfilled and impossible dream.

- Press the **Enter** key twice.

Now save the document on your exercise diskette giving it the filename MYFLY.DOC.

- Make sure your exercise diskette is in drive A.

- Select **File, Save,** or
  click the **Save** button on the toolbar, or
  press **Ctrl+S**.

- In the File Name box, type:

  a:myfly

- Click **OK** (or press **Enter**).

Opening a second document

At this point, you perhaps feel that another, existing document contains information that would be useful to check, add to or modify for this new document. To open a second document you can use the **File, Open** option, or **Open** button on the toolbar, as usual.

- Open the file A:HISTORY.DOC from your exercise diskette.

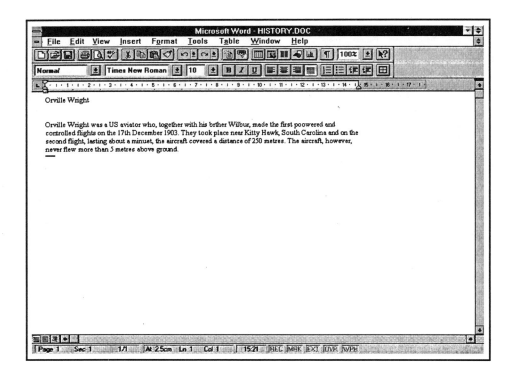

Your first document is hidden behind the new document. You can now use this second document window in exactly the same way as when you work with a single document.

Switching documents

To switch between two documents you can press **Ctrl+F6**, or open the the **Window** menu which will list the available document windows.

- Click on the MYFLY.DOC option in the Window menu, or press **Ctrl+F6**.

Your latest document starting <u>Those Magnificent Men</u>, is displayed again.

Arrange All

The **Window, Arrange All** option splits the screen to show both documents at once.

- Select the **Window, Arrange All** menu option.

Both documents are now on view (see picture on next page).

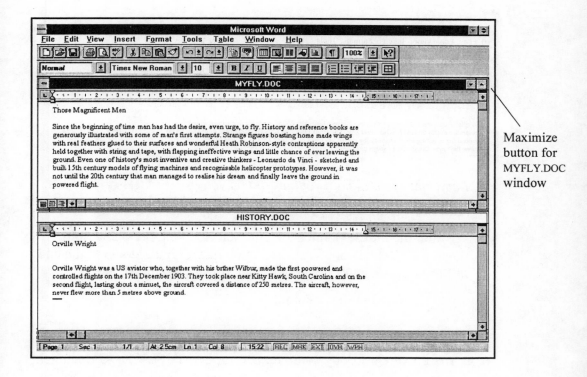

Maximize button for MYFLY.DOC window

Maximizing a document window again

Notice that both windows have become smaller. Each document window can be enlarged by clicking its **Maximize** button, the picture above shows the **Maximize** button for the MYFLY.DOC document window. When you select the HISTORY.DOC window its **Maximize** button will appear.

- Click anywhere on the HISTORY.DOC window to make sure that it is active.

- Click the **Maximize** button for the HISTORY.DOC document.

The HISTORY.DOC document will now fill the screen.

Copying text from one document to another

Assume the document relating to the Wright brothers contains text that would be useful to copy into your other document. To achieve this, you must first select the desired text and then move the block, switching windows as you go. Using drop and drag, you can drag selected text over from one window to another.

- Select the **Window, Arrange All** menu option again.

Now prepare the MYFLY.DOC document:

- Make the MYFLY.DOC window active by clicking on it and move the cursor to the end of the document (**Ctrl+End**).

- Now select the whole of the main paragraph about the Wright brothers in the HISTORY.DOC document.

☞ *Remember that to copy a block of text you use the* **Ctrl** *key, otherwise the block will be moved not copied.*

- Position the mouse pointer over the selected text, press and hold down the **Ctrl** key and drag the dotted insertion bar down to the end of the MYFLY.DOC document, then release the mouse button.

The text is inserted in the document.

Exercise

As an extra exercise, copy some text from the MYFLY.DOC document over to the HISTORY.DOC document, using Copy and Paste. The following steps will act as a guide.

- Highlight the first two sentences of the first paragraph.
- Copy the text (**Edit, Copy** or **Ctrl+C**).
- Switch documents (**Ctrl+F6**, or click on the document).
- Position the cursor at the desired point of insertion.
- Paste the text (**Edit, Paste** or **Ctrl+V**).

Ending the session

- Make sure the HISTORY.DOC document is displayed.
- Select **File, Close**, do not save the changes.

The MYFLY.DOC document should now be displayed.

- Select **File, Close**, do not save the changes.
- Select **File, Exit**.

Printing & Print Preview

You have already created and printed a few documents in earlier chapters without changing any settings. The Print option, however, offers a number of very useful alternatives - you can print out the whole of your current document, just the page you are currently working on or specifically selected pages of the document. The Print menu also enables you to check, amend or change your printer installation.

In this chapter, you will learn some of these features.

- Make sure your printer is on and ready to print.

- Start your Word program.

- If the Tip of the Day dialog box is displayed, read the tip and then click **OK**.

You should now have an empty document window.

- Make sure your exercise diskette is in drive A.

- Select **File**, **Open**, or
  click the **Open** button on the toolbar, or
  just press **Ctrl+O**.

The Open dialog box is displayed.

- In the File Name box, type:

  a:printing

- Click **OK**, or press **Enter**.

A document about printers is opened for you. It is several pages long.

Using the Print button on the toolbar

 If you remember, you can use the **Print** button on the toolbar to quickly print out the current document using the current settings. No Print dialog box is opened, the printout goes ahead automatically.

- Click the **Print** button on the toolbar.

☞ *If somebody else has changed any of the default settings, you may not get what you expect!*

The document is printed according to the current settings.

Choosing what to print

You can choose to print the whole document, the current page, selected pages, left or right pages only, or both, and more. All this is done via the Print dialog box.

Printing the current page only

During the course of your work, you may create a longer document, edit it and print it out, then make alterations on a single page. It is not always necessary to re-print the whole document. You can, therefore, choose to print out single or selected pages only.

- Select **File**, **Print**, or press **Ctrl+P**, but <u>do not</u> use the **Print** button on the toolbar this time.

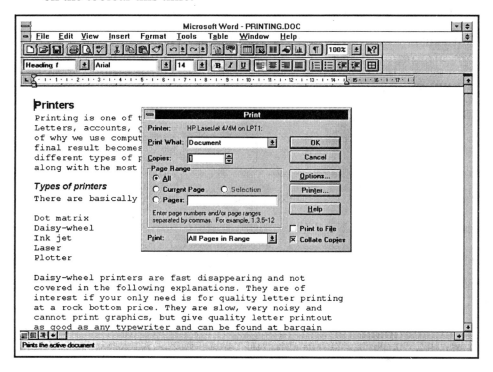

- Click the **Current Page** option.

- Click **OK**.

The current page only will be printed.

Printing selected pages

You can also print selected pages. Page ranges can be separated by commas, for individual pages, or by a hyphen for a continuous range, e.g. 2-3 or 2,5,8 Try printing pages 2-3 as follows:

- Select **File**, **Print**.

- Click the **Pages** option.

- In the Pages box beside the option, type:
  2-3

- Click **OK**.

Pages 2-3 will be printed.

How many copies?

The copies box allows you to print multiple copies of a document.

- Select **File**, **Print**.

- Click the **Current** option.

- In the Copies box, type:
  3

- Click **OK**.

The current page will be printed 3 times.

More printing options

There are several further print options available. For now, just inspect them as follows:

- Select **File**, **Print**.

- Click **Options**.

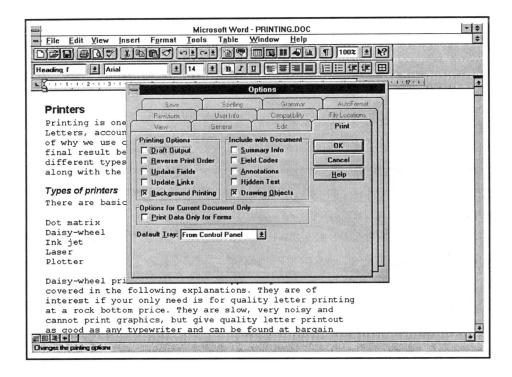

Inspect the options available.

- Click **Cancel** to close the Options dialog box. without making any changes.

- Click **Cancel** again, to close the Print dialog box.

Selecting a printer

If you have more than one printer installed, you can easily select the desired printer.

- Select **File**, **Print**.

- Click **Printer**.

A list of available printers is displayed and you could select one of them, but don't do so now.

- Click **Cancel** to close the Printers dialog box. without making any changes.

- Click **Cancel** again, to close the Print dialog box.

Previewing a document

To see what your document will look like, without the necessity of printing it out, you can use the **Print Preview** option to advantage.

• Select **File, Print Preview**, or click the **Print Preview** button on the toolbar.

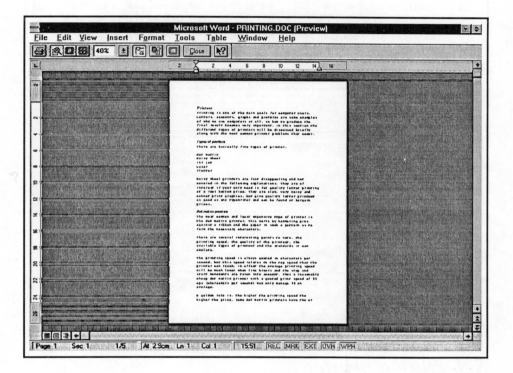

After a moments pause, your current document will be displayed. Several options are available including:

☺ If your document runs to several pages, you can scroll through the document (flip through the different pages) by using the **Page Up** and **Page Down** keys.

☺ You can click the **Print** button in the toolbar to print the document.

☺ Use the **Multiple Pages** button to view several pages at once and the **Single Page** button to view one page at a time.

⊕ You can click anywhere on the document with the Magnifying glass pointer to enlarge and reduce the display size.

• Press **Page Down** and **PageUp** to move between the pages.

 • Click the the **Multiple Pages** button (shown left) - a small box opens beneath it representing small pages.

• Position the mouse pointer over the second left square in the second row (i.e. 2 x 2 pages), then click the mouse button.

The following picture is an example of the display shown for multiple pages on an SVGA screen:

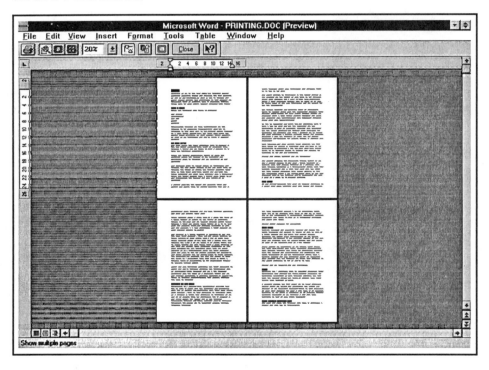

• When you are ready, click **Close**, to exit Print Preview.

Ending the session

• Select **File, Close**, do not save any changes.

• Select **File, Exit**, to exit Word.

Fonts and Styles

Word for Windows allows you to apply a variety of styles to the characters and words that make up your text. Each individual character can be formatted, although most often you will apply formatting to words or phrases. For example, you can mark text as **bold**, underlined, *italic*, subscript or superscript.

Word for Windows also allows you to format whole paragraphs and the page in general, but these features will be covered in the next chapters.

☞ *Formatting characters can mean a single character, a few consecutive characters, a word, a phrase, a sentence, or several sentences.*

☞ *Remember also that you can quickly use the* **Bold**, **Italic** *and* **Underline** *buttons in the toolbar, or their short-cut key equivalents,* **Ctrl+B**, **Ctrl+I** *and* **Ctrl+U**.

• Start Word and open FEAR.DOC from your exercise diskette.

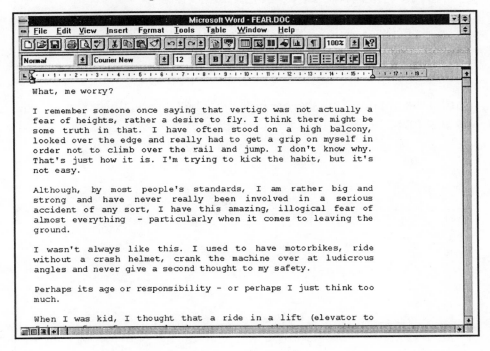

Formatting a phrase

Now have a go yourself:

- Select the phrase in the first paragraph <u>desire to fly</u>.

- Select **Format, Font**.

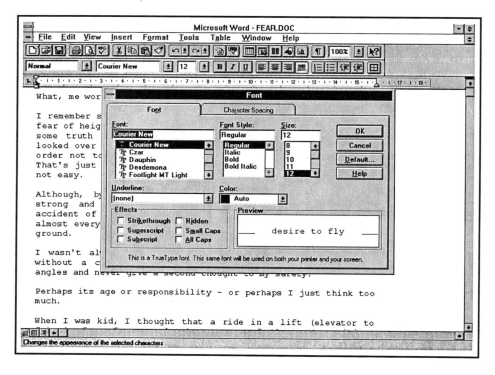

Most of the options available are obvious. The table on the next page will describe them.

Option	Description
Font	Choose a font from the list of available fonts, e.g. Times, Arial, Courier, Windings - ✈📄◆✉.
Font Style	Select the style for the font, e.g. Regular, **Bold**, *Italic*, ***Bold Italic***.
Size	Select a font size, measured in points, e.g. 8pts, 12pts, 18pts, 24pts.
Underline	Set the underline style, e.g. single, double, words only not spaces, dotted.
Effects	Choose special effects, e.g. ~~Strikethrough~~, Super script, Subscript, Hidden, SMALL CAPS, ALL CAPS.
Colour	Select a colour.
Preview	The Preview box shows a sample of the text with the settings you have chosen.

☞ *The font name, size and colour will depend on the capabilities of your printer. You will see how to select these later on in this chapter.*

☞ *Hidden text gives you the option of actually hiding a piece of text so that it is not seen on the screen or printed out. This might be, for example, a useful way of making some 'private' notes at relevant parts of your text.*

The hidden text function in the **Format**, **Font** *option marks the the selected text as hidden, it may or may not actually hide it. To decide whether hidden text is to be hidden or remain visible, a selection is made in the* **Tools**, **Options**, **View** *options.*

• Click the **Strikethrough** option so that it is crossed.

If you now look in the Sample box, you will see a sample of how your selected text will be affected.

• Click the **Strikethrough** box again to remove the cross.

- Click the **All Caps** option so that it is crossed.
- Select the **Bold** font style.
- Click **OK**.
- Click anywhere on the document to remove the selection highlight.

The text DESIRE TO FLY is now displayed in capitals and bold.

Clearing a format

You can reset characters to the default normal style using **Ctrl+Spacebar**. If the selected text has more than one format feature applied to it, e.g. strikethrough, bold and italic, then you can also remove any one of the formats by marking the text and de-selecting the formatting feature.

- Re-select the phrase DESIRE TO FLY.
- Press **Ctrl+Spacebar**.
- Click anywhere on the document to remove the selection highlight.

The characters are returned to the default style.

Changing fonts

Two of the options available via **Format, Font** are font name and font size. You can apply these to individual characters or words, or to a whole document. The quickest way of changing the font and its size is by using the list boxes available in the toolbar.

- Select the main heading What, me worry? (tripleclick on it).
- Select **Format, Font**.
- In the Fonts list, select **Arial**, or another available font.
- In the Font Style list, select **Bold Italic**.
- In the Size list, select **18**, or another available size.
- Check the Preview box to see the effects of your formatting.
- Click **OK**.

The heading is now formatted according to your settings.

- Click on the document to remove the selection highlight.

Using the toolbar

Fonts and font sizes can also be set using the Font and Size boxes in the toolbar.

- Select the phrase <u>kick the habit,</u> in the first paragraph.

- Click on the **Arrow** button beside the Font box in the toolbar.

You will be presented with a list of available fonts.

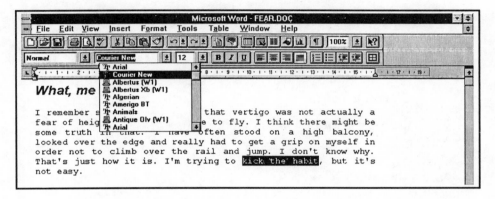

- Click one of the available fonts.

The font for the selected phrase has been changed. Keep the phrase selected for now.

- Click on the **Arrow** button beside the Size box in the toolbar to open the list of font sizes.

- Click one of the available font sizes - **14** if it is there.

- Click anywhere on the text to remove the selection highlight.

The new font size has been applied to the selected phrase.

- Click on the document to remove the selection highlighting.

Experiment

- Try changing the font and font size a few times for different sentences and phrases.

☝ *When you change fonts and sizes, you may want to check your document using the* **File**, **Print Preview** *option, since changes in font will affect how much can fit on a page.*

Superscript and subscript

You will now try writing H_2O and $3x^2$.

- Move the cursor down to the end of the document (**Ctrl+End**).

- Create a couple of empty lines if necessary.

- Type, with a few spaces between the two parts:

  H20   3x2

- Select the 2 in H20.

- Select **Format**, **Font**.

- Click the **Subscript** option so that it is crossed.

- Click **OK**.

- Now select the 2 in 3x2.

- Select **Format**, **Font**.

- Click the **Superscript** option so that it is crossed.

- Click **OK**.

You should now have achieved your goal.

- Try some more superscripts and subscripts of your own, but using the short cut key combinations **Ctrl+=** (Control and equals sign) for subscript and **Ctrl+Shift+=** for superscript.

Speed formatting keys

There are a number of speed formatting keys, or short cuts, available. It is up to you whether you wish to remember some of the short cuts for frequently used styles. Remember that bold, italic and underline are most easily activated using the respective buttons on the toolbar. An extended list is provided on the next page for your reference.

Format	Speed keys
Bold	**Ctrl+B**
Italic	**Ctrl+I**
Underline	**Ctrl+U**
Word Underline	**Ctrl+Shift+W**
Double underline	**Ctrl+Shift+D**
Small caps	**Ctrl+Shift+K**
All caps	**Ctrl+Shift+A**
Change case of letters	**Shift+F3**
Hidden	**Ctrl+Shift+H**
Subscript	**Ctrl+=**
Superscript	**Ctrl+Shift+=**
Back to normal, remove all formats	**Ctrl+Spacebar**

Using the short cut keys

The sequence of instructions for using the short cut keys is as follows:

⊛ Select the text you want to format.

⊛ Press the desired key combination.

☞ *Note that it is possible to combine two or more options at once by holding down the* **Ctrl** *key, or* **Ctrl+Shift** *keys, and pressing the desired short cut keys in sequence.*

- Select the text <u>That's just how it is</u> (in 1st paragraph).

- Press **Ctrl+Shift+D**.

- Click on the document to remove the selection highlight.

This text should now have a double underline.

- Select the text <u>I have often</u> (in 1st paragraph).
- Press **Ctrl+U, B**.
- Click on the document to remove the selection highlight.

Ending the session

When you are ready, close the document without saving the changes.

- Select **File, Close**, do not save the changes.
- Select **File, Exit**, to exit Word.

Formatting Paragraphs

There are a number of styles that you can apply to paragraphs; alignment, line spacing, indents and pagination, etc. You can format a single paragraph by positioning the cursor within the paragraph you want to format, or use one of the methods described in an earlier chapter to extend the selection to include several paragraphs.

In this chapter you will learn the basics. In later chapters, you will learn about borders and shading and about many of the Word features designed to speed up your work such as templates, AutoFormat and Wizards.

• Start Word and open PRINTING.DOC from your exercise diskette.

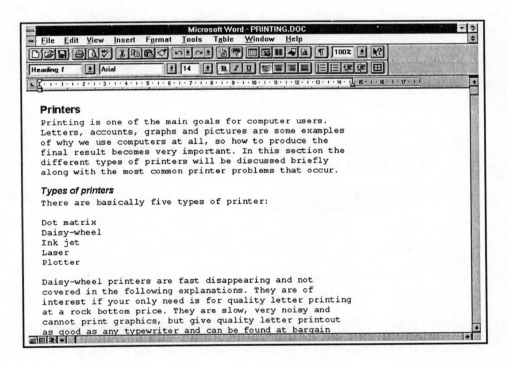

Paragraph alignment

The four alignment options are summarised below.

Alignment	Short cut keys	Description/Example
Align Left	**Ctrl+L**	The paragraph has a straight left-hand edge and ragged right-hand edge - normal setting.
Center	**Ctrl+E**	All text centred on each line.
Align Right	**Ctrl+R**	The paragraph has a ragged left-hand edge, straight right-hand edge.
Justify	**Ctrl+J**	Both left-hand and right-hand edges, apart from the very last line if it is short, have straight edges. Spacing between words is often adjusted to achieve this.

Short-cut buttons in the toolbar

There are four very useful short-cut buttons in the toolbar to help you quickly format paragraphs. The buttons are in the following order from left to right: **Align Left, Center, Align Right, Justify**.

- Position the cursor anywhere in the first paragraph.

- Click the **Align Right** button, to see the effect of right-aligning the paragraph.

- Click the **Center** button, to see the effect centring the paragraph.

- Click the **Justify** button, to see the effect justifying the paragraph.

- Click the **Align Left** button, to left-align the paragraph again.

Indents

You can indent a paragraph so that it is further in than the normal left or right margin.

 Once again, there are two useful short-cut buttons in the toolbar. Pictured here, they decrease or increase the indent respectively.

- Position the cursor anywhere in the first paragraph.
- Click the **Increase Indent** button (second of the two buttons).

Notice how the whole paragraph is shifted inwards.

- Click the **Increase Indent** button again.

The whole paragraph is shifted inwards one tab position more.

- Click the **Decrease Indent** button.
- Click the **Decrease Indent** button again.

The paragraph is moved back.

☞ *The position of the tab markers affects the indent feature. You will learn more about setting tabs in a later chapter.*

Bullets

 You can assign a bulleted indent to a paragraph. For example, all the instructions in this training course are bulleted with a dot. The short-cut **Bullet** button pictured here will automatically create a bulleted indent using the current default values.

- Click anywhere in the text <u>Dot matrix</u>, in the list of types of printers.
- Click the **Bullet** button.

The paragraph is indented with a dot as the bullet. Repeat this for the other printer types.

- Select the next four printer types in the list.
- Click the **Bullet** button.

Changing the bullet character.

It is possible to change the bullet to one of many characters and symbols.

- Select the five paragraphs in the list of printer types.

- Select **Format, Bullets and Numbering**.

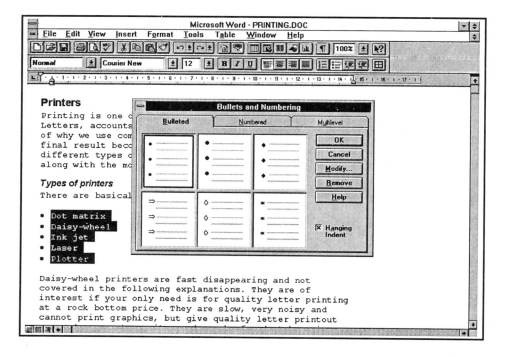

- Click the fourth bullet type, showing arrows as the bullet.

- Click **OK**.

- Click on the document to remove the selection highlight.

The bullets are now shown as arrows. Change them back again:

- Select the five paragraphs in the list of printer types again.

- Select **Format, Bullets and Numbering**.

- Click the first bullet type, showing dots as the bullet.

- Click **OK**.

- Click on the document to remove the selection highlight.

Removing bullets

To remove a bullet, you select the paragraph(s) with a bullet to be removed, and then click the **Bullet** button.

- Select the five paragraphs in the list of printer types again.

- Click the **Bullet** button.

- Click on the document to remove the selection highlight.

Lists of numbered points

In much the same way as creating bulleted indents, you can easily create paragraphs as a list of numbered points. Once again there is a short-cut button in the toolbar - as pictured here.

- Select the five paragraphs in the list of printer types again.

- Click the **Numbering** button.

- Click on the document to remove the selection highlight.

The paragraphs are numbered 1 to 5.

- Remove the numbering by selecting the paragraphs and clicking the **Numbering** button again.

Modifying bullets and numbered paragraphs

It is possible to modify bullets and numbered paragraphs in many ways - the indent, the bullet, the type of number, etc. To do this, you should select the desired paragraphs, then select **Format, Bullets and Numbering,** and then click the **Modify** button. A range of options is available for you to modify. The options are not covered here.

Line spacing

Normally your paragraphs will be single spaced - there will be no blank lines between the lines within a paragraph. You can, however, set any number of lines if you require. Other standard spacings are one-and-a-half and double line spacing.

- Position the cursor anywhere in the first paragraph.

- Select **Format, Paragraph**.

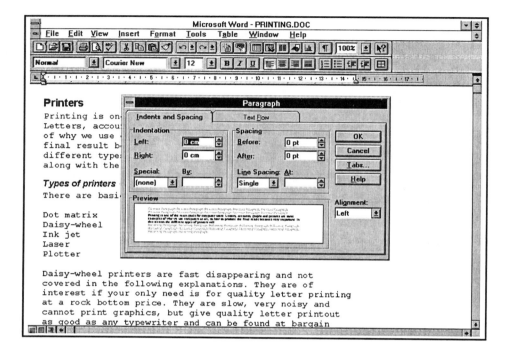

The Paragraph dialog box is opened. You will see many options including indents and alignments, that can be set here rather than using the buttons in the toolbar.

- Click the Line Spacing: At: box to open the list of pre-defined line spacings.

- Click the **Double** option.

- Click **OK**.

Note the effect on the paragraph.

- Select **Format, Paragraph** again.

- Click the Line Spacing: At: box.

- Click the **1.5 Lines** option.

- Click **OK**.

Experiment

- Experiment a little now, changing the alignment, line spacing and indentation of various paragraphs. Add a bullet or two as well!

- When you are ready, select **File, Close** and do not save the changes.

Aligning text as you go

This section will give you a little practise at formatting paragraphs as you go. Start of by opening a new document.

- Click the **New** button.

- Click the **Center** button.

The paragraph marker will now be positioned in the middle of the current line. Any text that you type in will spread out on either side.

- Type:

Mr & Mrs Ponsonby-Smythe

- Press **Enter** twice.

Notice how the centred format continues to be applied to new paragraphs.

☞ *Important principle:*
Whenever you press **Enter** *to conclude a paragraph, the format of the paragraph you are concluding is carried forward and will apply to the new paragraph. You can of course alter the format of the new paragraph if you want to.*

- Type:

Request the pleasure of your company

- Press **Enter** twice.

- Type:

at the saddling of their foal

- Press **Enter** three times.

- Set the alignment to right by clicking the **Align Right** button.

- Type:

  Please reply promptly to:
  Kendrick Hall
  Kendrick Park
  CIRENCESTER
  Glos.

- Press **Enter** three times.

- Set the alignment back to left by clicking the **Align Left** button.

- Click the **Numbering** button.

- Type:

  Remember our rules!:

- Click the **Numbering** button.

- Type (noting that the numbers appear automatically):

  No animals
  No smoking
  Don't be late

Ending the session

Finish off by closing the current document.

- Select **File, Close** and do not save the changes.

- Select **File, Exit** to exit Word.

Page Layout

In addition to using the various character and paragraph formats to enhance your document, you may need to, or simply wish to, make overall adjustments to the size of your page and the margins around it. For instance, in order to make page breaks work properly, Word for Windows will need to know the size of paper you are using. Furthermore, you can greatly enhance the effect of your documents by choosing suitable margins to create space around your text.

This chapter covers the margin options and how to create headers and footers, i.e. text that is automatically repeated at the head (top) and foot (bottom) of each page. You will also learn about adding the date and how to force a page break.

Some other options, such as Paper Source and Paper Size, will be looked at, but not tested.

- Start Word, you should have an empty document window to start with.

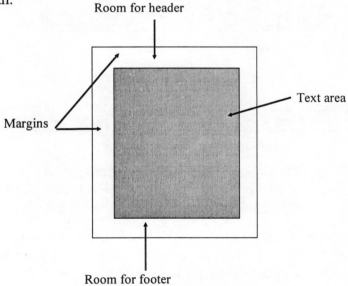

Room for header

Text area

Margins

Room for footer

Page Setup options

When setting up you page, there are some important components to think about; the page size and orientation, the margins and the paper source options. All of these options are covered in the **File**, **Page Setup** menu option, which you will investigate now.

•   Select **File**, **Page Setup**.

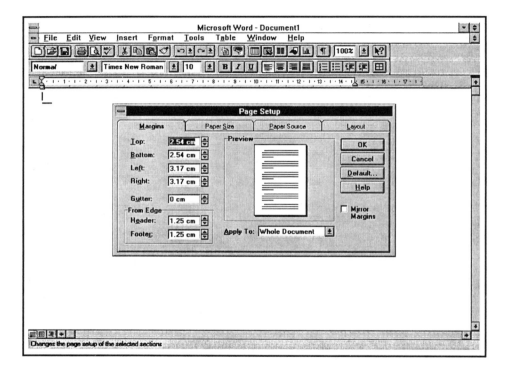

The Page Setup dialog box has four different sections; Margins (currently shown), Paper Size, Paper Source and Layout. Each section is represented rather like a card file - click the desired card to show the options.

☺   Each set of options has an Apply To box where you can decide whether to apply any changes you make to the whole document or only from the current cursor position onwards.

☺   There is also a **Default** button. This can be used to set up any of the options as the default settings for Word.

⊛ Each set of options also has a Preview box to show you what you page will look like if you apply the changes you make.

• If necessary, click on the **Margins** tab - on the actual wording.

You can set the top, bottom, left and right margins. Also, you can set the gutter, which is an extra non-writing area on the edge of the page (for example, to allow for the holes in your course file), or between two pages if the document has facing pages.

• Click on the **Paper Size** tab - on the actual wording.

• Study the options, but do not make any changes.

The page size is limited by the size of the paper you are using in your printer. It is important to give Word for Windows the correct settings. If you are using 11" paper, and tell Word for Windows that your paper is 12" long, do not be surprised if the printing extends over the perforations!

You can choose the paper size from the list in the Paper Size list box, or adjust the size manually. You can also chose the orientation, either portrait or landscape.

• Click on the **Paper Source** tab - on the actual wording.

• Study the options, but do not make any changes.

The Paper Source options allow you to choose from which paper tray the paper should come. The options will depend on your printer. You can choose to have the leading sheet from one tray and the following sheets from another. This is very useful when you have two trays, one of which contains letterhead paper.

• Click on the **Layout** tab - on the actual wording.

• Study the options, but do not make any changes.

Notice in particular, that you can choose to have different headers and footers for odd and even pages, and for the first page.

• Finally, click **Cancel** to close the Page Setup dialog box.

Margins

In order to see the effect of changing the margins, you will start off by opening one of the files on your exercise diskette.

- Open the file PRINTING.DOC form your exercise diskette.

- Select **File**, **Page Setup**.

- If necessary, click the **Margins** tab.

As mentioned, there are four margins you can set - left, right, top and bottom. Generally speaking about 1" will look appropriate on 11", 12" or A4 paper, and still leave you room for simple headers and footers such as page numbers or chapter titles.

- Enter the following values:

Top margin	**3"** (or 7.5 cm)
Bottom margin	**2"** (or 5 cm)
Left margin	**1.5"** (or 4 cm)
Right margin	**1.5"** (or 4 cm)

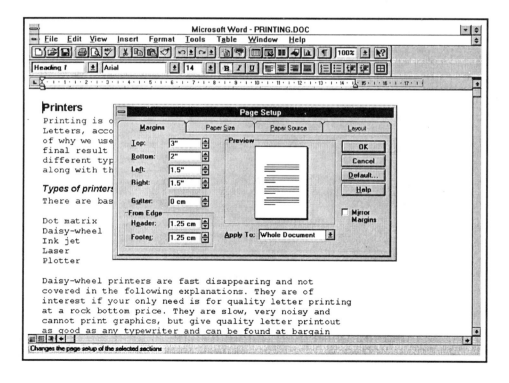

☞ *Note that you can type in inches or centimetres regardless of the current units of measurement. Just type, for example, 3" or 3 in or 3 cm. Next time you open the Margins options, the measurements will have been automatically converted to the current units.*

* Click **OK**.

The text will be adapted to fit the new page size and margins.

☞ *If the Normal view is selected just now, you may only notice a slight difference in the amount of text that fits in per line. The change to the top and bottom margins doesn't show.*

Now check the effect of changing the margins by using Print Preview.

* Click the **Print Preview** button on the toolbar, or select **File**, **Print Preview**.

* Click the **One Page** button in the toolbar, if necessary, to show one page at a time.

* Use **PageDn** to scroll through the pages.

* Use the **Multiple Pages** button to view the pages 2 x 2.

* When you are ready, click **Close**.

Headers and Footers

A running head (header or footer) is a piece of text that is printed at the top or bottom of every page. Obvious examples would be the chapter title (see the top of this page) and page numbers (see the bottom of this page).

Headers and footers are very similar, apart from their position, that is. Both can have a different first page, for example, a title page, and can be set up to have different headers and footers on the left and right sides.

In Word for Windows headers and footers are like any other paragraph and text - and can be centred, justified, include bold, etc.

* Select **View**, **Header/Footer**.

A dotted rectangle is shown in which you can create your header. There is a small window with various buttons for you to use.

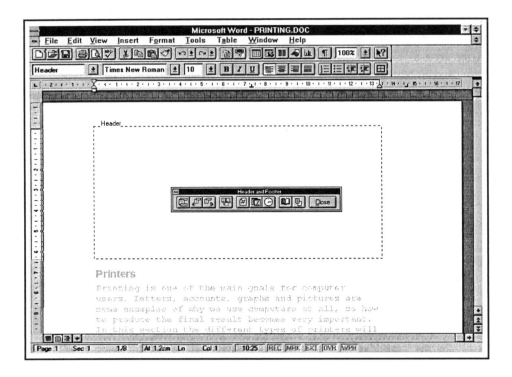

- Move the mouse pointer slowly over the Header & Footer buttons, without clicking on them, to see what each button does.

Adding a header

Now add a header to the document.

- Type:

    Printers

- Centre the paragraph by clicking the **Center** button in the toolbar (or press **Ctrl+E**).

Adding a footer

Now create a footer to include the page number.

- Click the **Switch Between Header and Footer** button, the first of the buttons in the small Header and Footer window.

A Footer section at the bottom of the screen is now shown.

- Type (with a space at the end):

  Page

- Centre the paragraph by clicking the **Center** button in the toolbar (or press **Ctrl+E**).

Inserting a page number

To insert the current page number you simply click the Page button (#).

- Click the **Page Numbers** button (5th button).

- Click **Close**.

The header and footer are now complete.

Page Layout view

To view the result, the Page Layout view is ideal. This shows the pages as they will be printed, including the header and footer. You may or may not already have the Page Layout view selected.

- Open the **View** menu and click the **Page Layout** option.

- Use the **PageDn** key to scroll through the text - you will notice the header and footer on each page in a lighter coloured text.

- Print out the document, pages 1-2 only.

Changing the header and footer

Headers and footers can be edited as normal text.

- Select **View, Header and Footer**.

- Change the header to read:

  All About Printers

- Switch to the footer.

- Move the cursor to the end of the footer text and press **Enter**.

- Click the **Date** button (6th button).

- Click **Close**.

The header and footer have now been revised.

- Use the **PageUp** and **PageDn** keys to scroll through the text again, noting the change.

- Print out the document, page 3 only.

Forcing page breaks

You can force Word to make a page break anywhere in the document by pressing **Ctrl+Enter**.

- Move the cursor to immediately before the <u>D</u> in the heading <u>Dot matrix printers</u>.

- Press **Ctrl+Enter**.

A page break is inserted immediately and the heading is moved to the top of the next page.

Page breaks in the Normal view

In the Normal view, forced page breaks are shown by a line across the page. Other page breaks are shown by a dotted line across the page.

- Open the **View** menu and click the **Normal** option.

- Use the **PageUp** and **PageDn** keys to scroll through the text again, noting the different page breaks.

Ending the session

- Select **File**, **Close** and do not save the changes.

- Select **File**, **Exit** to exit Word.

The Spelling Checker & Word Count

The Spelling Checker is a very useful tool when you need to check your document for spelling mistakes. The Word Count feature will quickly tell you how many characters and words your document contains.

Using the Spelling Checker

The spelling checker in Word is both simple to use and very fast. It rapidly scans your texts to ensure that you have not made any spelling errors or typing errors and checks for duplicates, i.e. the same word twice in a row. Any words that it does not recognise are immediately highlighted and possible alternatives to the word in question are suggested.

You should, however, bear in mind that no spelling checker is infallible, neither is it the answer to all your problems. Questions of style or word usage cannot be checked. For example, if you use the word **there** instead of **their**, providing it is spelt correctly the spelling checker will not draw your attention to the mistake.

The spelling checker will sometimes highlight a word although it is spelt correctly. This may simply be due to the fact that the word has not been included in the standard Word dictionary, but you can add words to the dictionary as you go.

The spelling checker always carries out its check on the current document, i.e. the document that is displayed in active document window. So, to practise using the spelling checker, you must give it something to work with! You will now load the file SPELLCHK.DOC from your exercise diskette. The document has a few deliberate mistakes already made for you!

- Start Word.

- Open the file SPELLCHK.DOC from your exercise diskette.

The SPELLCHK.DOC document is now displayed on your screen and is ready to be checked. As usual, there are several different ways of starting the Speller:

- Select **Tools**, **Spelling**, or
  click the **Spelling** button on the toolbar, or
  press **F7**.

The spelling checker immediately swings into action and highlights the word <u>posibility</u> in the first paragraph.

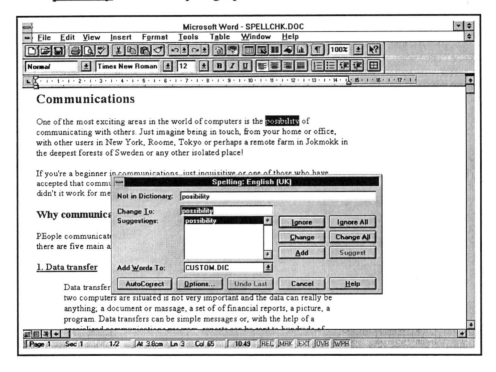

Notice that the Change To box contains a suggestion of how to correct the word - in this case, the correct spelling <u>possibility</u>.

Speller offers you several options. The table on the next page describes the the main options that are available.

Option	Description
Ignore/Ignore All	Skip any changes to the highlighted word and carry on with the next check - Ignore All also skips any further occurrences.
Change/Change All	Change the highlighted word to the currently selected alternative - Change All also changes all further occurrences.
Add	Add a word to the selected custom dictionary.
Suggest	Ask Word to suggest an alternative word - this is only active if the Always Suggest option is turned off.
Cancel	Quit the spelling checker program.
AutoCorrect	This feature is covered in a later chapter and allows you to set up Word to automatically correct certain mistakes.
Options	Allows you to change some default settings.

- Click **Change All** to replace the word in the document with the word in the Change To box, and every other occurrence of the mis-spelling.

The next problem is the word <u>Roome</u>, which is a mis-spelling of Rome. Word correctly analysed this and suggests you change it to <u>Rome</u>.

- Click **Change**.

The spelling checker next highlights the word <u>Jokmokk</u>, which is in fact a small town in North Sweden, but Word doesn't recognise it! You can ignore this problem.

- Click the **Ignore** button.

The next problem is the word <u>PEople</u>,which has two capital letters at the start instead of one. Again Word picks this problem out and suggests the correct alternative.

- Click **Change**.

Word now points out a repeated word, <u>if </u>appears twice in a row by mistake.

- Click **Delete** to delete the repetition.

The next problem is the word <u>tiimes,</u> which is mis-spelt.

- Click **Change**.

Now Word questions the word <u>entertainments,</u> but on consideration it is OK.

- Click **Ignore**.

The next problem is the missing space in <u>withouthaving</u>. There are no suitable alternatives for you to select, so you have to change the word directly in the Change To box.

- In the Change To box, position the cursor between <u>without</u> and <u>having</u>.

- Press the **Spacebar** to insert a space.

- Click **Change** to confirm the correction.

The spelling check is now complete and you are finally asked to click OK.

- Click **OK**.

Word count

As an added bonus, Word can do a word count for you.

- Select **Tools, Word Count**.

Word informs of the number of pages, words, characters, paragraphs and lines in your document.

- When you are ready, click **Close**.

Ending the session

- Select **File, Close** to close the current document, do not save the changes.

- Select **File, Exit** to exit Word.

The Thesaurus & Grammar Checker

This chapter presents a short introduction to two more useful tools for proofing your documents, the Thesaurus and the Grammar Checker.

Thesaurus

If you are stuck for a word, or a particular synonym, a thesaurus is a very useful feature to have at your finger tips. A thesaurus is, quite simply a dictionary of synonyms that can help you find a more suitable alternative to a particular word. Of course, the most comprehensive thesaurus is in book form, but Works offers you a reasonable alternative to working your way through that thick volume, if you can find it in the first place that is!

- Start Word.

- Open the file THES.DOC from your exercise diskette.

At the end of the document there is a list of five words for which you have to find alternatives.

- Place the cursor anywhere on the first word <u>melancholy</u>.

- Select **Tools**, **Thesaurus**, or press **Shift+F7**.

The Thesaurus dialog box is opened displaying a selection of words to choose from.

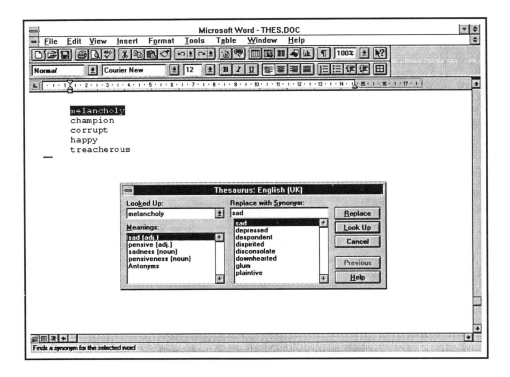

Suppose that a suitable alternative is <u>downhearted</u>.

- Select the word <u>downhearted</u> in the Replace with Synonym list.

- Click **Replace**.

The dialog box is closed and the change is made automatically in your document.

Now find another word for <u>champion</u>.

- Place the cursor anywhere on the word <u>champion</u>.

- Select **Tools**, **Thesaurus**, or press **Shift+F7**.

The Thesaurus dialog box is opened again. Looking at the list of alternatives, suppose you choose <u>conqueror</u>.

- Select the word <u>conqueror</u> in the Replace with Synonym list.

- Click **Replace**.

The dialog box is closed and the change is made automatically in your document.

- Place the cursor anywhere on the word <u>corrupt</u>.

- Select **Tools**, **Thesaurus**, or press **Shift+F7**.

Looking at the list of alternatives, suppose you decide that <u>corrupt</u> was the best alternative after all, so that no replacement is needed:

- Click **Cancel**.

Look up

When you use the thesaurus to suggest a synonym, as you did in the above examples, you can actually look up synonyms of synonyms to provide you with a larger range of alternatives.

The best way to show this is by an example. Suppose you want to find a much stronger alternative for the word <u>happy</u>:

- Position the cursor anywhere on the word <u>happy</u>.

- Select **Tools**, **Thesaurus**, or press **Shift+F7**.

Looking at the list of synonyms, you think that <u>delighted</u> is getting closer to what you want:

- Select the word <u>delighted</u> in the Replace with Synonym list.

- Click **Look Up**.

A new list is now shown.

- Select the word <u>ecstatic</u> in the Replace with Synonym list.

- Click **Replace**.

Once again the change is made automatically in your document.

Meanings

In the final example, you will find an alternative for the word <u>treacherous</u>, but assume that the meaning is <u>travelling in treacherous conditions</u>.

- Place the cursor anywhere on the word <u>treacherous</u>.

- Select **Tools**, **Thesaurus**, or press **Shift+F7**.

This time, look at the Meanings box; There are two alternative meanings, <u>traitorous</u> and <u>unreliable</u>. In our case, we clearly mean <u>unreliable</u>.

- Select the word <u>unreliable</u> in the Meanings list.

As usual, the list of synonyms is updated, try finding a suitable alternative:

- Select the word <u>difficult</u> in the Replace with Synonym list.

- Click **Look Up**.

The new list of synonyms is presented, but the synonyms are not suitable.

- Click **Previous**.

- Select the word <u>unreliable</u> in the Meanings list again.

- Select the word <u>unstable</u> in the Replace with Synonym list.

- Click **Look Up**.

Once again the synonyms are not suitable.

- Click **Previous**.

- Select the word <u>unreliable</u> in the Meanings list again.

- Select the word <u>insecure</u> in the Replace with Synonym list.

- Click **Look Up**.

This time the word **unsafe** is in the list, and you decide to select it.

- Select the word <u>unsafe</u> in the Replace with Synonym list.

- Click **Replace**.

You have now finished testing the Thesaurus.

- Select **File**, **Close** and do not save the changes.

Grammar checker

The grammar checker is very useful for picking up further errors in your document. For example, it will spot when you use *its* instead of *it's*, incorrect verb forms and incomplete sentences to name but a few. At the end of a grammar check, it will also supply you with some interesting statistics.

- Open the GRAMCHK.DOC document from your exercise diskette.

- Select **Tools**, **Grammar**.

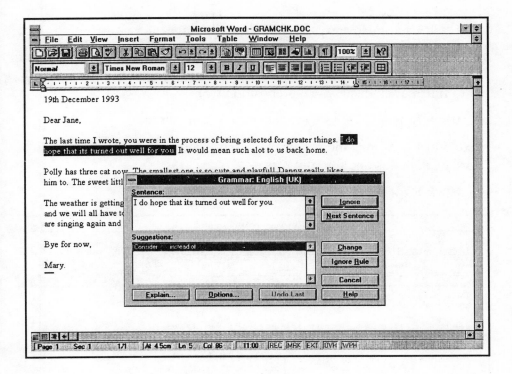

The grammar checker swings immediately into action. The first error it spots is the incorrect use of <u>its</u>. This is shown in the Sentence box. In the Suggestions box, the alternative <u>it's</u> is suggested, which is correct.

• Click **Change**.

Next it picks up <u>alot</u> which of course should be <u>a lot</u> as suggested.

• Click **Change**.

Word now picks up a possible spelling error and opens the Spelling checker - it doesn't like the word **Polly**.

• Click **Ignore**.

The next sentence with an error is <u>Polly has three cat now</u>. Although it is obvious that <u>cat</u> should be <u>cats</u>, this is not the problem highlighted just now. Word doesn't like the sentence, but let's say it's OK.

• Click **Ignore**, to ignore the suggestion from Word.

Now Word picks up the <u>cats</u> mistake.

- Click **Change** to carry out the selected change.

The next sentence with an error is <u>Danny really likes him to</u>. This time, Word does not pick up the fact that <u>to</u> should be <u>too</u>, but advises you instead not to finish a sentence with a preposition (<u>to</u>).

- Click **Ignore**, to ignore the suggestion from Word.

Next Word questions the use of the passive voice in <u>is often forced</u>. Let Word explain this one for you:

- Click **Explain**.

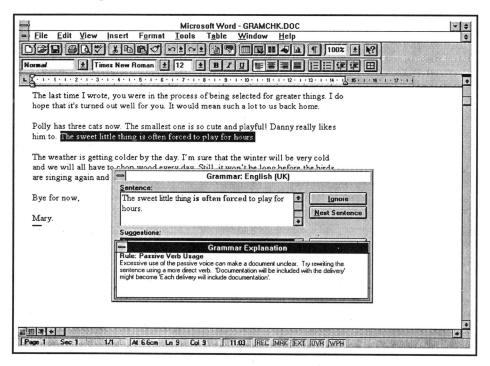

The Grammar Explanation dialog box is opened with an explanation of the passive verb usage. In our case, the passive verb has not been used excessively and does not need changing.

- Click the Control menu box of the Grammar Explanation dialog box and select **Close** (or just doubleclick the Control menu box).

- Click **Ignore**, to ignore the suggestion from Word.

Next Word suggests <u>I am</u> instead of <u>I'm</u>.

- Click **Ignore**, to ignore the suggestion from Word.

Next Word suggests <u>will not</u> instead of <u>won't</u>.

- Click **Ignore**, to ignore the suggestion from Word.

In the last main sentence, Word picks out <u>children runs</u>. In the suggestions box, two alternatives are suggested; <u>child instead of children</u> and <u>run instead of runs</u>.

- Click on the second suggestion, <u>run instead of runs</u> to select it.

- Click **Change** to carry out the selected change.

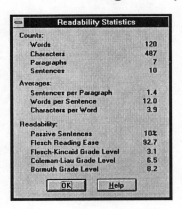

The grammar check is now complete and you are presented with a set of statistics. Apart from the number of words, characters, paragraphs and sentences, there are other figures that relate to the readability of your document.

- When you are ready, click **OK**.

Ending the session

Finally, close the document without saving the changes - this will allow you to repeat this exercise later, if you wish to do so.

- Select **File**, **Close**, do not save the changes.

- Exit Word.

Find & Replace

The **Find** function is an invaluable editing aid when you need to search for one or more occurrences of a word or phrase in your document. The **Replace** function enables you to search for a word or phrase and replace it with a different word or phrase.

To see how these functions work in practice, you will need a document to work on.

- Start Word.

- Open the file STARTUP.DOC from your exercise diskette.

Find

When searching for a word, phrase or string of text, using Find or Replace, there are certain things you can control.

- Select **Edit, Find** (or press **Ctrl+F**).

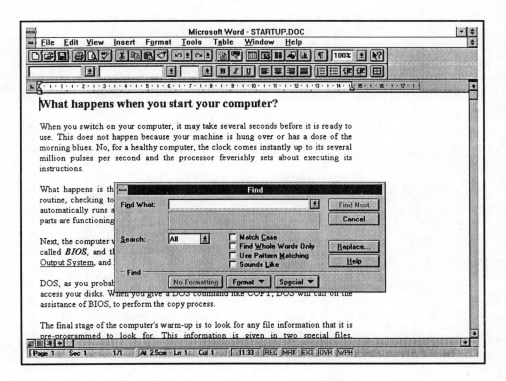

The Find dialog box is opened. The following table briefly explains these possibilities.

Type	Description
Search All/Down/Up	Choose whether to search the whole of the document (All), from the cursor position downwards (Down), or from the cursor position upwards (Up).
Match Case	Determines whether particular notice of upper and lower case letters should be taken. For example, for the purposes of the search, is **Hello** the same as **HELLO**.
Find Whole Words Only	Determines whether to find whole words only or not, e.g. finding 'it' could be construed as finding for the word 'it' only, or any occurrence such as 'itch' or 'whiter'.
Use Pattern Matching	Advanced search criteria, not covered in this course.
Sounds Like	Searches for words that sound like the word you want to find as well as those that match it, e.g. **color** and **colour**.
Format	These options allow you to search for formats and styles.
Special	Reveals a list of special characters you can search for, e.g. paragraph marker, tab marker, manual page break.

Assume that you need to search for the word <u>BIOS</u>.

- In the Find What box, type:

  bios

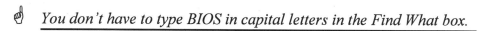 *You don't have to type BIOS in capital letters in the Find What box.*

- Make sure the **All** option is selected in the Search box.

- Click **Find Next** to start the search.

The cursor immediately moves to the position where the word <u>BIOS</u> first occurs.

- Click **Find Next** again.

The cursor moves to the next position where the word occurs.

- Click **Find Next** again.

The next occurrence is found.

Ending the search

To end the search, simply click **Cancel**.

- Click **Cancel**.

Find - another example

Assume that you want to find the word <u>DOS</u> in your document. You may realise in advance that other words can include dos in them, e.g. dose, doses, dossier. In order to find just DOS, you could either type it in the Find What box in capital letters and then set the Match Case option, or you could set the Whole Words Only option.

- Move the cursor to the beginning of the document (**Ctrl+Home**).

- Select **Edit**, **Find** (or press **Ctrl+F**).

Notice that the previous search word, <u>bios,</u> is still in the Find What box.

- In the Find What box, type:

  dos

- Click the **Find Whole Words Only** option so that it is crossed.

- Click **Find Next** to start the search.

The first occurrence is found.

- Click **Find Next** again and then again, to find the next occurrences.

Now cancel the search:

- Click **Cancel**.

Replace

This feature allows you to search for a specific word, or group of words, and replace it with another, different word, or group of words. Try replacing the word <u>monitor</u>, with the word <u>screen</u>.

- Move the cursor to the beginning of the document (**Ctrl+Home**).

- Select **Edit**, **Replace**, or press **Ctrl+H**.

Notice that the Replace dialog box is slightly larger than the Find dialog box. It has a Replace With box, and **Replace** and **Replace All** buttons. The **Find Next** button is still there, so the Replace feature can still be used to find words.

- In the Find What box, type:

  monitor

- In the Replace With box, type:

  screen

There are two ways of replacing text:

① Use **Find Next** to find the next occurrence, then click **Replace** to do the replacement, or if you don't want to perform the replacement this time, click **Find Next** again to skip over it.

② Use **Replace All** to automatically replace all occurrences.

In this case, you can happily replace all occurrences automatically. In another document, you might have to think if you have used the word <u>monitor</u> with another meaning, e.g. "he was asked to monitor her progress".

Doing an automatic replacement would yield "he was asked to screen her progress".

- Make sure that the **Find Whole Words Only** option is selected.

- Click **Replace All**.

Word carries out all the replacements and opens a dialog box to tell you how many times.

- Click **OK**.

- Click **Close** to close the Replace dialog box.

Undoing a Replace All

If you realise that you have made a mistake replacing all occurrences, you can immediately undo the changes.

- Select **Edit, Undo Replace All**, or press **Ctrl+Z**.

The replacements are reversed.

Replace - a second example

In this example, you will replace the word computer with PC, although not all occurrences.

- Select **Edit, Replace**, or press **Ctrl+H**.

- In the Find What box, type:

  computer

- In the Replace With box, type:

  PC

☝ *By typing in PC in capitals, you will automatically force Word to use PC in capitals when replacing the word computer.*

- Click the **Find Whole Words Only** option so that it is not crossed.

Because you don't want to change all occurrences, you will have to find each one and then choose whether to replace it or not.

- Click **Find Next**.

The cursor moves to the first occurrence in the title. Choose not to replace it by moving on to the next occurrence.

- Click **Find Next**.

The cursor moves on to the next occurrence. This time replace it:

- Click **Replace**.

The replacement is made and the next occurrence automatically found.

- Carry on through the document, deciding yourself whether to re-place each individual occurrence or not.

When the end of the document is reached Word will tell you how many replacements were made.

- Click **OK**.

- Click **Close** to close the Replace dialog box.

Replacing with styles

In this final example, you will find all the occurrences of the word **DOS** and apply a style to them.

- Move the cursor to the beginning of the document (**Ctrl+Home**).

- Select **Edit**, **Replace**, or press **Ctrl+H**.

- In the Find What box, type:
  DOS

- In the Replace With box, type:
  DOS

- Make sure the **Find Whole Words Only** option is crossed.

Now set the format features that you want to apply.

- Click on the Replace With box to make sure it is active.

☝ *It is important to make sure the Replace With box is selected, if the Find What box was selected instead, then you would set the format features to find, rather that the format features to replace.*

- Click the **Format** button and select **Font**.

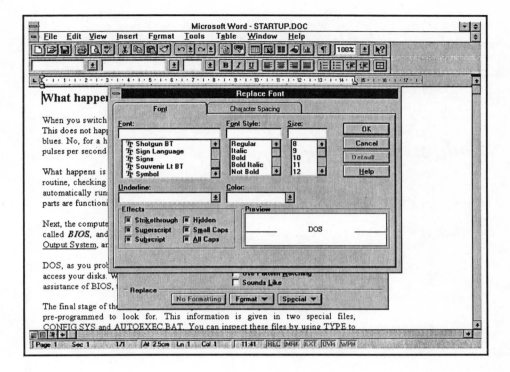

The Replace Font dialog box is opened (not the Find Font dialog box!)

- In the Font Style list, click the **Italic** option.

- In the Sizes list, select a smaller font size, say **8**.

- Open the Underline list box and select **Double**.

- Click **OK** to close the dialog box.

You are now ready to start the replacement.

- Click **Replace All**.

Word carries out all the replacements.

- Click **OK**.

- Click **Close** to close the Replace dialog box.

☝ *If you carry out a second replacement without closing the Replace dialog box, the formatting features selected will remain selected even for the next replacement. This may produce unwanted results! Closing the Replace dialog box, however, clears the selected options.*

Ending the session

- Try a few replacements of your own.

- Select **File, Close**, and do not save any changes.

- Select **File, Exit**, to exit Word.

Using Tabs

Tab stops are often used to line up information in a document and to create simple tables. You would probably use the Table feature to create larger tables and this is covered in the next chapter. When using tabs, you can either use the default tab stops set every 0.5 inches (or 1.27 cm), or set up your own tab stop positions. In this chapter, you will see one example of each.

- Open the FOOTBALL.DOC file from your exercise diskette.

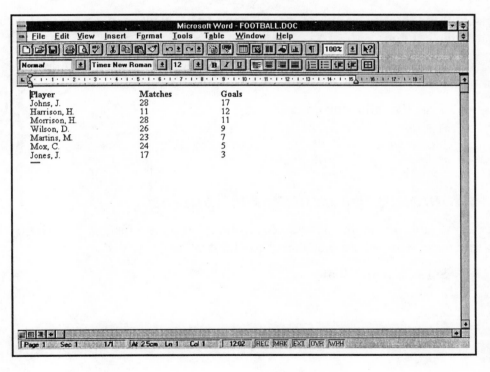

When dealing with tabs, it is useful to display the non-printing characters:

- Click the **Show/Hide P** button on the toolbar.

As you can see now, this simple table has been created by typing in some information and lining up the columns using differing amounts of tabs (shown as →).

The Ruler

The Ruler, just above the text area in the document window, will probably be set to show inches or centimetres. All measurements in the instructions that follow will state both inches and centimetres and you should select them as appropriate.

The Ruler also has a button on its left-hand edge. Clicking the button will change the button itself to show what sort of tab is currently selected. You will learn more about this later in the chapter.

Adding some more entries

Now add three more entries, pressing the **Tab** key where necessary to line up the columns.

- Move the cursor to the end of the document (**Ctrl+End**) and press **Enter** to start a new line.

- Type the following entries:

Wise, K	14	3
Loveshore, J	21	2
Pates, P	19	1

Changing the default tab spacing

In the table above, the default tab positions (every 0.5 inches, or 1.27 cm) are used. You will now change the default tab width to 0.7".

- Select **Format, Tabs**.

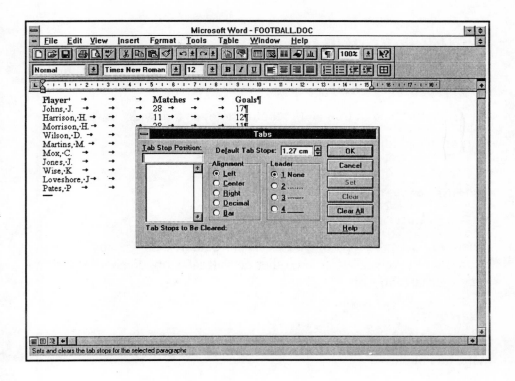

- Clear the entry in the **Default Tab Spacings** box.

- Type:

  0.7 in (or 1.7 cm)

- Click **OK** (or press **Enter**).

Each tab now moves along accordingly. As you can see, this has disrupted the appearance of the table, which shows the value of using your own custom tabs when doing tables! Finish off by closing the document.

- Select **File, Close**, do not save the changes.

☞ *For some small tables, the default tabs may be appropriate, in which case it is probably easiest to use them. In other cases, it is wiser to set up your own tab stops, as described in the next section.*

Setting your own tab stops

You will now open a new file and create a price list, with an item number, a description and a price.

- Click the **New** button on the toolbar to open a new document.

Start off by adding a line of text:

- Type:

   Price List 1993/94

- Press **Enter** twice to move the cursor down.

When you set tab stops of you own, the default tabs are automatically cleared up to your tab stop, but other default tab stops remain in position after your last tab stop.

Alignment

Each tab stop can be set up with a particular alignment. These are described in the table below.

Table type	Description
Left	Left end of text aligned to tab stop
Centre	Text is centred on tab stop
Right	Right end of text aligned on tab stop
Decimal	Decimal point aligned on tab stop

Using the Ruler

The quickest way to set a tab stop is to click on the Ruler. The alignment of the tab you add will depend on the currently active tab on the left hand edge of the Ruler. Now try adding a left aligned tab at 1.5" (4 cm) and a decimal tab at 4" (10 cm).

- Make sure the tab type on the left-hand edge of the Ruler is **Left** (see picture), if not, click the Tab Type button until it is Left.

- Click on the Ruler, on the 1.5" (4 cm) mark.

A tab marker shows the tab stop position.

- Click the Tab Type button 3 times, until the Decimal tab type is displayed.

- Click on the Ruler again, on the 4" (10 cm) mark.

Another tab marker should appear.

Entering text

Now add some details to the table:

- Type:

  Item No

- Press the **Tab** key.

- Type:

  Description

- Press the **Tab** key.

- Type:

  Price

- Press the **Enter** key.

The top of your document should now look like this:

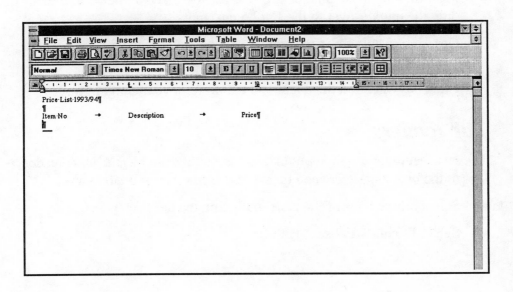

You can now add some more details. Enter the following lines of information, pressing the **Tab** key to move between the columns and the **Enter** key at the end of each line.

- Type:

D101	Domestic polish	£24.50
D102	Domestic wax	£17.35
S220	Coat hangers	£12.30
X203	Dusters	£9.25
X402	Anti static pads	£11.00

Your table is complete for now. If you want to add more entries later on, do so as an additional exercise.

Moving a tab marker

It is very simple to move a tab marker. Assume that you want to move the 1.5" (4 cm) tab marker back to the 1" (2.5 cm) mark.

 If you move a tab marker, only the current paragraph will be affected. You need to select the whole table to change it all.

Proceed as follows:

- Select all the lines of the table, including the headings (drag the mouse down the selection bar alongside the table to highlight it).

- Position the mouse pointer over the 1.5" (4 cm) tab marker and then drag the marker over to the 1" (2.5 cm) mark.

The Description column in the table is changed to line up with the new tab stop position.

- Click anywhere on the document text to remove the highlight.

Tab leaders

The last feature you will apply in this chapter is called a *leader*. A leader fills in the blank space created before text is lined up at a tab marker.

- Select all the lines of the table, including the headings.

- Select **Format, Tabs**.

In the Tab Stop Position list, you will now see the 1" (2.5 cm) and 4" (10 cm) tabs are there.

- In the Tab Stop Position list, click on **4" (10 cm)**.

You can now alter the settings for this tab position.

- Click on option **3** in the **Leader** group of options.

- Click **OK** (or press **Enter**).

A line is filled in between the <u>Description</u> and <u>Price</u> columns.

- Click anywhere on the document text to remove the highlight.

Ending the session

- Experiment a little more with tab positions and their markers.

When you have finished:

- Click **Show/Hide P** button to hide the non-printing characters.

- Select **File**, **Close** to close the document, do not save the changes.

- Exit Word.

Tables

Word has a very simple table feature that will help you create tables quickly and easily, without the bother of setting tab positions. Tables can be used for figures, text or a combination. There is also a *Table Wizard* to help you automate the process of creating a table.

- Make sure you are starting with a new document.

- Type the following heading:

  Product Sales 1992/93

- Press the **Enter** key twice.

Creating a table

You can insert a new table anywhere in your document at the cursor's position. The **Insert Table** button is shown on the left.

- Click the **Insert Table** button.

You will notice that a table grid is displayed. By dragging the mouse you can decide the size of the table, i.e. the number of rows and columns.

- Start at the first top-left square and drag the mouse down and to the right until you have selected a 5 x 6 Table, i.e. 5 rows and 6 columns (see picture below) - then release the mouse button.

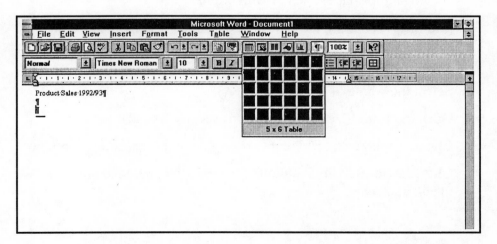

You have now created an empty table.

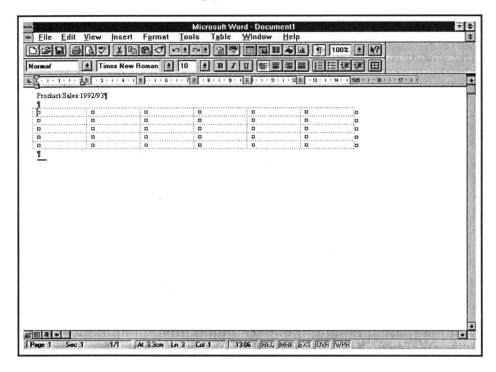

Cells

Every table is made up of cells. In each cell you can type text or numbers and even insert graphics. The contents of each cell, or a block of cells, can be selected and formatted, just as with ordinary text.

The grid lines separating the cells are not printed when you print out your document - they are there for your guidance only. It is possible to hide the grid lines, which you may want to do to see how the table looks.

- Select the whole of the text (**Ctrl+A**).

- Open the **Font Size** box in the toolbar and select size 12.

- Click anywhere on the document to remove the selection highlight.

- Click the **Show/Hide P** button, if necessary, to hide the non-printing characters.

Entering text/numbers

To move between the cells, you can simply click on the desired cell, or use the **ArrowKeys**.

• Type in the information shown in the picture below.

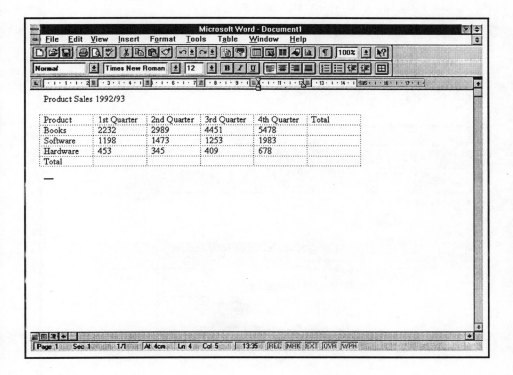

Save the table

• Make sure your exercise diskette is in drive A.

• Select **File, Save**, or
  click the **Save** button in the toolbar, or
  press **Ctrl+S**.

• In the File Name box, type:

  a:mytable

• Click **OK** or press **Enter**.

Using formulae

In your table so far, you have not added up the different totals. You don't need to do this by hand, you can use Word's Formula function to help you. Try calculating the sum of the first row of figures as follows:

- Select the last cell in the <u>Books</u> row.

- Select **Table**, **Formula**.

The Formula dialog box is opened. The Formula box already suggests that it should calculate the sum of all the figures to its left using the formula =SUM(LEFT).

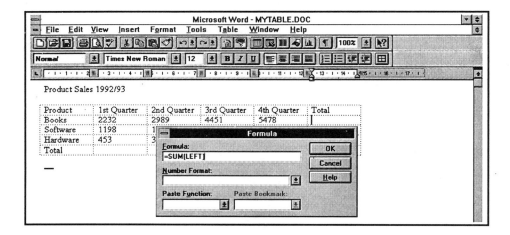

- Click **OK** to confirm the suggested formula.

The total, <u>15150</u>, is filled in automatically. If you change any of the values in the row, the total is not recalculated automatically - try it:

- Select the first value in the <u>Books</u> row and change it to 1999.

Note that the row total is not updated.

- Select the last cell in the <u>Books</u> row.

- Select **Table**, **Formula**.

- Click **OK** to confirm the suggested formula.

The row total is now updated.

Filling in the other row totals

Now repeat the above instructions to fill in the other row totals:

- Select the last cell in the Software row.

- Select **Table, Formula**.

This time Word suggests the formula =SUM(ABOVE), which is wrong as you need the sum of the figures to the left of the cell.

- Change the formula to:

  =SUM(LEFT)

- Click **OK** to confirm the suggested formula.

The Software row total is now calculated.

- Select the last cell in the Hardware row.

- Select **Table, Formula**.

Again Word suggests the wrong formula.

- Change the formula to:

  =SUM(LEFT)

- Click **OK** to confirm the suggested formula.

The Hardware row total is now calculated.

Calculating the column totals

The next step is to calculate the column totals in exactly the same manner.

- Select the last cell in the 1st Quarter column.

- Select **Table, Formula**.

This time Word suggests the desired formula =SUM(ABOVE).

- Click **OK** to confirm the suggested formula.

The 1st Quarter column total is now calculated.

Exercise

- Repeat the process yourself for the remaining column totals.

- Click the **Save** button, or press **Ctrl+S** to save the document.

Formatting a table

You can now set about formatting the table. Start off with the heading first.

- Select the heading Product Sales 1992/93.

- Click the **Bold** and then **Center** buttons, then select a **14pts** font size.

Now format the first and last rows of the table:

- Select the whole of the first row of the table.

- Click the **Bold** button (or press **Ctrl+B**).

- Select the whole of the last row of the table.

- Click the **Bold** button (or press **Ctrl+B**).

Right-aligning the numbers

The numbers in the table would be better if they were right-aligned.

- Select all the table cells containing numbers.

- Click the **Right** alignment button.

Hiding and displaying the gridlines

The gridlines in the table are for guidance only. You can hide them to see what the table will look like when printed.

- Select **Table, Gridlines**.

The gridlines are hidden.

- Select **Table, Gridlines** again.

The gridlines are displayed again.

Inserting a new row

You will now change the table to insert a new row at the top and then join some cells together. The picture below will give you an idea of what you are about to do.

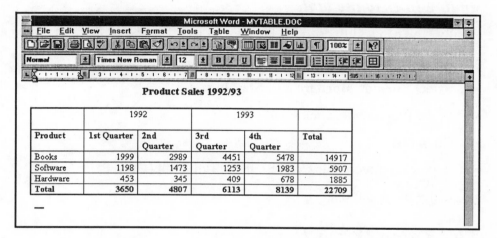

- Select the whole of the top row of the table by clicking just to the left of the row in the selection bar.

- Select **Table, Insert Rows**.

You now have a new empty row at the top of the table. In this row, you will enter the actual year corresponding to the quarterly figures.

- In the second cell of the top row, type:

  1992

- In the fourth cell of the top row, type:

  1993

Merging cells

Some cells need to be joined together to complete the table formatting.

- Select the 2nd and 3rd cells in the top row of the table.

- Select **Table, Merge Cells**.

- While the merged cell is still selected, click the **Center** button.

- Select the 4th and 5th cells in the top row of the table.

- Select **Table, Merge Cells**.

- While the merged cell is still selected, click the **Center** button.

Adding lines to the table

Finally, you can add lines to the table as follows:

- Make sure that the cursor is in the table.

- Select **Format, Borders and Shading**.

- In the Presets box, click **Grid**.

- Click **OK**.

- Save your document (**Ctrl+S**), then print it out (**Ctrl+P**).

- Close the document.

The Table Wizard

Word has a special Table Wizard that will help you to create a table. Wizards in general are covered in a separate chapter later on.

- Open a new document.

- Select **Table, Insert Table**.

- Click the **Wizard** button.

The Wizard takes you through a few simple steps to help you create the table.

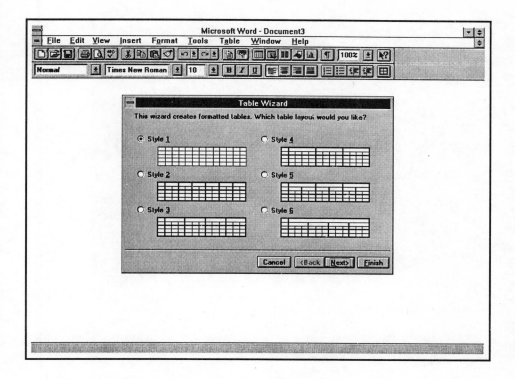

- Click **Style 6**.

- Click **Next**.

You will then be asked several more questions.

- Select **Year, quarters, then months** and click **Next**.

- Now click **Next** 5 times to accept the suggested options, or you can experiment by choosing different options.

- Finally, click **Finish** to finish creating the table.

Table AutoFormat

The last stage gives you the opportunity to format the table in advance. Word has an AutoFormat feature which lets you select one of many pre-programmed formats.

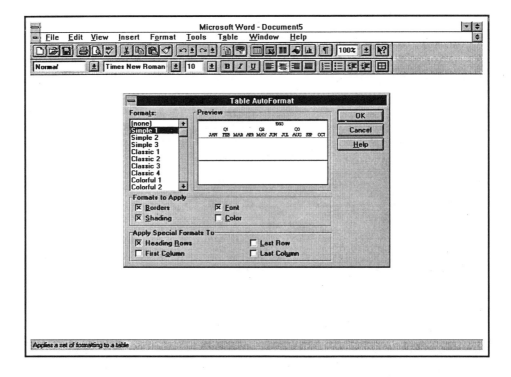

- In the Formats list, click the **Classic 2** option.

- Click **OK**.

The table is inserted into your document.

- Fill in a few imaginary figures.

Experiment

- Open a new document and use the Table Wizard to create a table of your own.

Ending the session

You have finished working tables for now.

- Close any open documents.

- Exit Word.

Newspaper Columns

Newspaper columns are the familiar style of columns found in a newspaper or newsletter. In this chapter, you will adapt the file COSTA.DOC.

- Open the COSTA.DOC file from your exercise diskette.

To set up newspaper columns, you can either use the short cut button on the toolbar, pictured left, or the **Format**, **Columns** menu option. The column format will take place from the cursor's position.

Using the Columns button

- Make sure the cursor is at the beginning of the document.
- Click the **Columns** button.

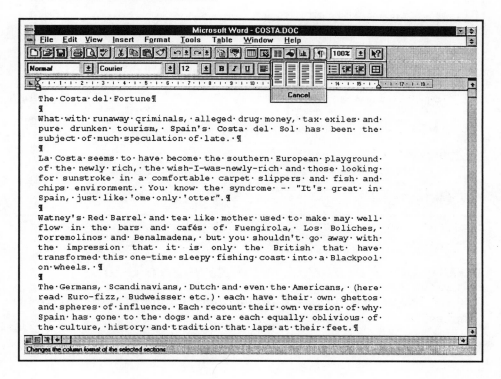

A small picture is displayed under the button showing four columns. If you click the first one, your document will have one column only. If you click the second one, you will get two columns, etc.

● Click anywhere on the third column.

To see the effect of the columns, you must use the page layout view.

● If necessary, select **View**, **Page Layout**.

Your document should now displayed with three columns.

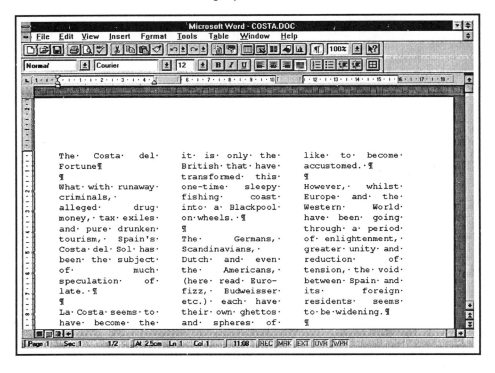

Using the Format, Columns menu option

You can also use the **Format**, **Columns** menu for more control over your columns.

● Select **Format, Columns**.

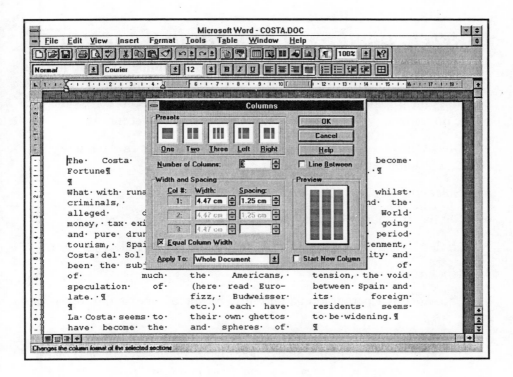

The Columns dialog box offers five preset columns, and various options that affect the number and sizing of columns. You can select the number of columns (up to 45!), the width of each column and the space between it and the next column, whether or not you want a vertical line between the columns, start a new column and finally what to apply the column settings to - this might be the whole document, a selected section or from the cursor's position onwards.

The current setting of three columns will be selected.

- Click the **Line Between** option so that it is crossed.

- Click **OK**.

Vertical lines should now be shown between the columns of your document.

Different numbers of columns in the same text

You can format the document to have all sorts of numbers of columns on the same page. You will now format the current document so that the heading and first paragraph are in a single column, spread across the top of the document, with the remaining text split into two columns.

- Select the text from the title down to the end of the first paragraph, and to include the empty paragraph.

- Select the **Format**, **Columns** option.

- Set the number of columns to 1 (click the first Preset option).

Notice that the Apply To option is automatically set as **Selected Text**.

- Click **OK**.

The title and first paragraph should now be spread across the top of the page.

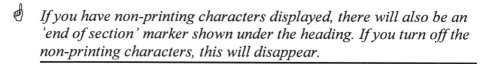 *If you have non-printing characters displayed, there will also be an 'end of section' marker shown under the heading. If you turn off the non-printing characters, this will disappear.*

Now adjust the title.

- Click anywhere on the title and click the **Center** button.

- Select the whole title and click the **Bold** button on the toolbar, and then use the **Font Size** button on the toolbar to select a font size of **24**.

Finally, adjust the remainder of the document to two columns only.

- Click on the beginning of the second paragraph.

- Select the **Format**, **Columns** option.

- Set the number of columns to 2.

The Apply To option is automatically set to **This Section**.

- Click **OK**.

- The top of the second column may now start with an empty line - if so, delete the empty line.

Shrink to fit

- Click the **Print Preview** button, or select **File**, **Print Preview**.

- Click the **Multiple Pages** button and select two pages wide by one page high.

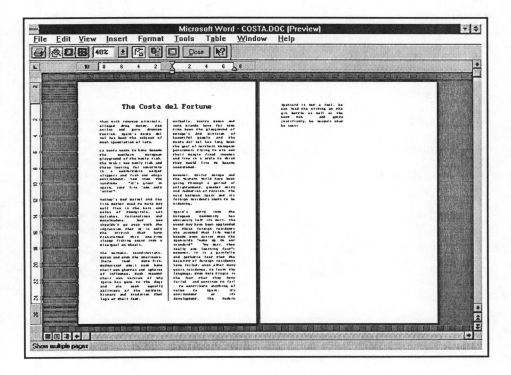

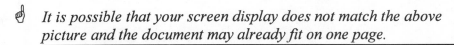

The document does not quite fit onto a page.

☞ *It is possible that your screen display does not match the above picture and the document may already fit on one page.*

- Click the **Shrink to Fit** button.

Word now attempts to fit the document onto one page less, i.e. in this case, on one page only.

- Click the **Print** button, to print out the document.

- Click **Close** to close the Print Preview window.

☞ *If you don't like the result of using the* **Shrink to Fit** *option, you can use* **Edit**, **Undo** *to reverse it.*

Ending the session

Now save the document on your exercise disk with a new filename MYNEWS.DOC.

- Select **File, Save As**.

- In the File Name box, type:

  a:mynews

- Click **OK**.

- Select **File, Close** to close the document.

- Select **File, Exit** to exit Word.

Documents and Directories

This chapter is the first of two that cover how to work with documents and directories.

You have already learned that in order for it to be possible to save texts and refer to them again at a future point in time, the texts must be given a filename and you have already created and named a number of documents.

A **document** is the actual text that you write and the paper copy you print out, while a **file** is the string of data making up your document, which is stored on a disk. However, it is often more convenient to use the terms document and file to mean the same thing - your text.

Listing files

If you have a large number of files or documents, it is not always possible to remember all their names or even where they are stored. You should always remember that although your computer is an admirable piece of equipment, it is not intelligent and is completely incapable of working on its own initiative. If, therefore, you wish to load a document you have named WORTH.DOC, but can only remember that it was called something that began with 'W', the computer cannot do it alone. If you try and retrieve a document called 'W', the computer does not have the intelligence to understand what you really want.

Sometimes you may find it difficult to find a document that you know DOES exist. This will happen if your document has been saved in one directory or drive, but you are searching in another.

- Select **File**, **Open**, or
  click the **Open** button in the toolbar, or
  press **Ctrl+O**.

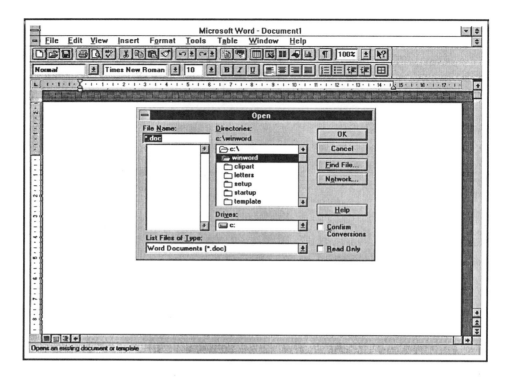

The Open dialog box should now be thoroughly familiar to you! A list of documents available in the **current directory** is displayed.

Changing drives

To change drives, just open the Drives list box by clicking on the arrow down symbol beside it, then select the desired drive.

- Make sure your exercise diskette is in drive A.

- Open the Drives list and click on **a:** to select drive A.

The documents on your exercise diskette will be shown in the list of files.

- Open the Drives list and click on **c:** to select drive C.

Changing directories

Each drive will have its own set of directories. Disk drives A and B will probably only have the root directory, but your hard disk will have several. The list of directories and their subdirectories is controlled by the Directories list box.

To change to the current directory, simply click the directory name.

- In the Directories list, doubleclick the **c:** option to make it the current directory.

☞ *The list of files may or may not be empty now.*

- Try doubleclicking a few more of the directory names in the Directories box.

- Click **Cancel** to abandon the Open command.

Listing selected files only

It is very simple to get Word to list selected groups of files only. This will be especially useful when the number of files has grown so that using the scroll boxes to locate files becomes tedious.

- Select **File**, **Open**, or
  click the **Open** button in the toolbar, or
  press **Ctrl+O**.

- Select drive A in the Drives list box.

The documents on your exercise diskette will be listed.

Normally, Word lists all the files in the current directory that have the extension .DOC. You can, however, list other files, or selected groups of files.

An asterisk * is used generally as a wildcard, that is it can be used to mean "any filename or part of a filename".

☞ *The wildcard system used in Word for Windows, using the asterisk *, matches the general DOS system of wildcards.*

The following table will help to explain more exactly what is meant.

Filename with wildcard	Description
.	Any file with any extension, i.e. all files
*.DOC	Any file with the extension DOC
HISTORY.*	Any file with the name HISTORY and any extension
HISTORY.DOC	Any file with the name HISTORY and the extension DOC, i.e. the file HISTORY.DOC
H*.DOC	Any file starting with H and with the extension DOC
H*.*	Any file starting with H and any extension

With this knowledge, we can make listing files much more comprehensible.

- Doubleclick the entry in the File Name box so that it is selected.
- Type:

  c*.doc

- Click **OK** or press **Enter**.

The list of files is updated to include only starting with C and with a .DOC extension.

Using the List Files of Type box

You can also use the List Files of Type box at the bottom of the dialog box.

- Open the list of file types in the List Files of Type box.
- Click the **All Files (*.*)** option.

The list of files is updated again.

- Open the list of file types in the List Files of Type box again.
- Click the **Word Documents (*.doc)** option.
- Finally, click **Cancel** to close the dialog box.

Opening documents not created in Word

You can open some files that have not been produced using Word for Windows. Documents from some applications can be converted and loaded. From other applications, the documents will need to be saved as ASCII files.

Loading a WordPerfect 5.1 document

A WordPerfect 5.1 file, ENGINE.LES is supplied on your diskette. Try loading it as follows.

- Make sure your exercise diskette is in drive A.

- Select **File**, **Open**.

- If necessary, select drive A in the Drives list box.

- Open the List Files of Type box and select **All Files (*.*)**.

- Locate and doubleclick the filename ENGINE.LES.

Word has automatically opens the WordPerfect 5.1 document.

Saving files as non-DOC

When you save a file, Word for Windows will automatically put a .DOC extension on the filename unless you specify a different extension (e.g. LETTER.TXT). However, the file will still contain all the special codes used by Word for formatting the document. If you want to save the file to be used by another word processor, you need to save it in the format required for that word processor, or in text-only format, although this will lose any special formats (bold, italic etc.) that you have used.

- Select **File**, **Save As**.

The Save File as Type list box contains a long list of document types. Normally this will be set to Word Document, but just now it shows **WordPerfect 5.1 for DOS**, because the file you opened was in that format. If you want to save the document in another format, you just select the desired format.

- Open the Save File as Type box and select the Windows Write format (towards the bottom of the list).

- Edit the filename in the File Name box to **engine.wri**.

- Click **OK**.

The file will be saved on the drive A, with its new filename and in its new format.

- Close the current document without saving the changes.

Merging files

Another possibility that Word offers is the ability to merge two files into one. This is very useful if you are working on something at home and something at work and wish to join the files together.

You will now merge two of the exercise files into one.

- Open the STARTUP.DOC

☞ *When merging two files, the second file is inserted into the first file at the current cursor position.*

Assume that we wish to tag the file MEMORY.DOC onto the end of the current file.

- Move the cursor down to the end of the text (**Ctrl+End**).
- Press **Enter** to create an extra empty line.
- Select **Insert, File**.
- Locate and doubleclick the filename MEMORY.DOC.

Now save the complete file with the name MERGED.DOC.

- Select **File, Save As**.
- In the Filename box, type:
  a:merged
- Click **OK** or press **Enter**.

Ending the session

- Close any open documents without saving the changes.
- Exit Word.

Using Find File

The Find File feature enables you to search for, copy, delete, open, print and preview files, and to work on groups of files. Find File can be selected via the File menu, or via the **Find File** button in the Open dialog box.

- Select **File**, **Open**.

- Click **Find File**.

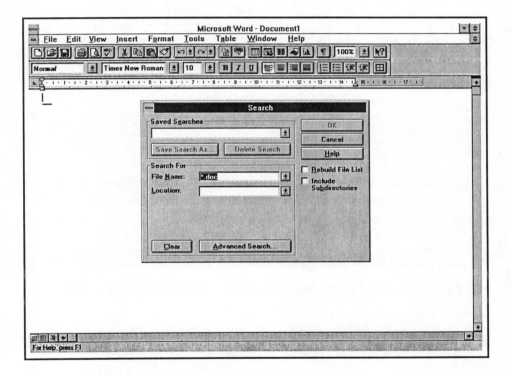

The Search dialog box is opened allowing you to tell Word what to look for and where to look. The Saved Search box will also contain a list of search criteria you may have saved.

- Open the Location box and click **a:** to select drive A.

- Click **OK** to start the search, which then takes a while to complete.

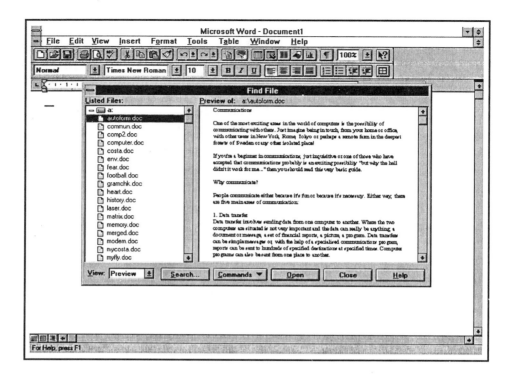

A list of the files in the selected drive and directory is displayed, along with the a Preview window for the selected file. You can select other files by clicking them or by using the **ArrowUp/Down** keys.

☞ *The list of files may be presented in a different order on your screen!*

- In the Listed Files list, click on the filename GRAMCHK.DOC to select it.

Standard features of Find File

Many standard features are available, each with its own button to click. The table on the next page shows a list of options available.

Feature	Description
View	Allows you to select the Preview, File Info or Summary view of the document.
Search	Returns you to the Search dialog box.
Commands	Opens a menu from which you can select the following: **Open as Read Only:** open a file as read only, i.e. can't be edited **Print:** Prints the selected file or group of files **Summary:** Edit the summary information for the selected file **Delete:** Deletes the selected file or group of files **Copy:** Copies the selected file or group of files **Sorting:** Allows you to sort the list of files in different ways
Open	Opens the selected file.
Close	Exits Find File.
Help	Opens the Help file.

Summary

By selecting the Summary option, you can edit the summary details.

- Click **Commands** and then select **Summary**.

Various information about the file is displayed and can be altered. There is also a **Statistics** button that will reveal statistical information about the contents of the file.

- Click the **Statistics** button.
- When you are ready, click **Close**.
- Click **Cancel** to close the Summary Info dialog box.

Sorting

Sorting allows you to change the content and order of the information displayed.

- Click **Commands** and then select **Sorting**.

The Options dialog box is opened.

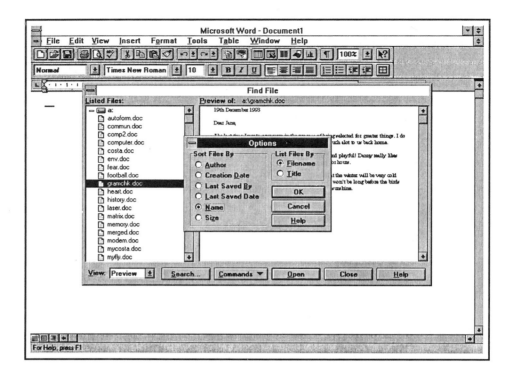

The Sort Files By options allow you to sort the list of files displayed in different ways. The List Files By options let you change the information that is displayed about the file.

- Click the **Size** option, then click **OK**, to sort the files in order of their size - again this will take a few moments to be completed.

The new list is presented. Now change it back:

- Click **Commands** and then select **Sorting**.

- Click the **Name** option, then click **OK**.

Opening a file in Find File

Find File can, naturally, be used to open files too.

- Select the file MEMORY.DOC in the list of files.

- Click **Open**.

The file is opened for you - close it now:

- Select **File, Close**.

Working with groups of files

One very useful feature of the Find File option is the ability to select several files at once for copying, printing and deleting.

• Select **File, Find File**.

The Find File dialog box is opened quite quickly, but you may notice that Word continues to work on the list for a while.

Selecting files

To select a file, just click on it. To select more than one file, hold down **Ctrl** and click on the files.

• Hold down **Ctrl** and click several files.

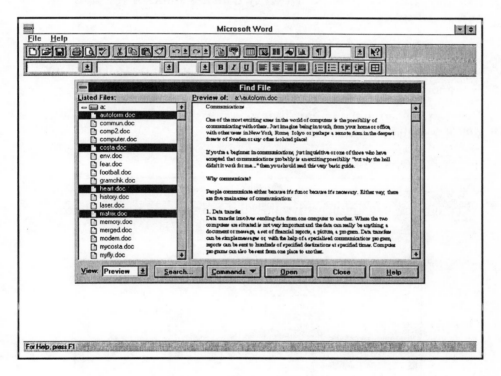

If you select the wrong file, you can de-select it by clicking on it again (still with **Ctrl** depressed).

• De-select one of the files you have just marked.

Once you have selected the files you want to work with, you can print, copy or delete all of them.

Printing a group of files

- Click the **Commands** button and select **Print**.

Find File opens the normal Print dialog box.

- Click **Cancel** to cancel the Print command for now.

The Find File dialog box is closed automatically.

Copying files

Once you have selected a group of files, you can copy them all to another existing directory or drive. Now try copying some of the files on your exercise diskette.

- Select **File, Find File**.

- Select the following files only: HEART.DOC, GRAMCHK.DOC and LASER.DOC.

You can now copy these three files to your C:\ directory (don't worry, you will delete them again soon!).

- Click the **Commands** button and select **Copy**.

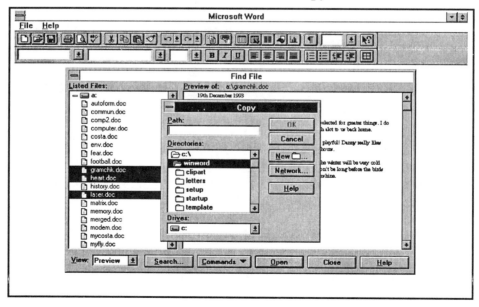

The Copy dialog box is opened.

- If necessary, open the Drives list and select **c:**.

- In the Directories list, click **c:**.

- Click **OK**.

The selected files will be copied.

Deleting files

Selected documents can be deleted very easily, so now delete the three files you copied in the exercise above.

- Click **Search** to return to the Search dialog box.

- Open the Location list and select **c:**.

- Click **OK**.

The list of files is updated.

☞ *Word will always select the first file in the list. If this file is not a Word file, you will get a message to this effect.*

- Select the following files only: HEART.DOC, GRAMCHK.DOC and LASER.DOC.

You can now delete these three files from your C:\ directory.

☞ *Before proceeding, double check that you have selected the correct three files.*

- Click the **Commands** button and select **Delete**.

As a precautionary measure, Word opens a dialog box asking you to confirm the deletion.

- If you are certain you have the correct files selected, click **YES** to go ahead with the deletion, otherwise click **No**.

Ending the session

- Now click **Close** to exit Find File.
- Close any open documents.
- Exit Word.

Styles, Templates and AutoFormat

Although you have already covered formatting paragraphs, Word has some very useful tools available to help you format paragraphs and documents very quickly and efficiently. In this chapter, you will learn about styles, templates and AutoFormat.

Paragraph styles explained

It is quite common to want to format paragraphs in different ways. Some paragraphs may be headings, others need indenting, others formatting in a special way, etc. Word has a convenient system to enable you solve this problem easily. Paragraph styles can be set up and named and any paragraph can then have the selected style automatically applied to it. As an example, you could set up a paragraph style as Garamond font, 24 point size, bold and italic, and call the style HeadG24. You could then apply this style to any paragraph in your document, presumably it would be certain titles or headings.

In this way, you can build up a set of paragraph styles and quickly format whole documents.

⊛   The default style for any paragraph is called **Normal**.

Templates explained

A template is a collection of paragraph styles, together with a set of page layout settings. By collecting these settings in unique template files (*.DOT), you can easily create different templates for different purposes.

Each document has a template assigned to it. You have already used the Normal template. When you start Word you are presented with a clear document which has automatically been assigned the Normal template.

Word has many pre-defined templates full of paragraph styles suitable for that type of document. With time, you may wish to create your own templates.

Using paragraph styles

The Style box is on the toolbar, furthest to the left, and will probably show **Normal** just now.

- Click on the arrow beside the Style box in the toolbar to open the list of styles.

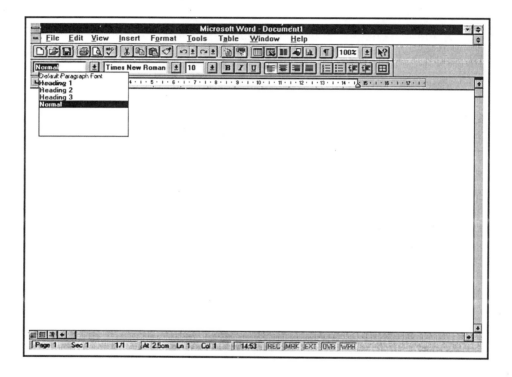

The styles **Heading1, Heading2** and **Heading 3** are available.

- Click anywhere on the document to close the Style box.

- Open the file STYLES.DOC from your exercise diskette.

The document contains the text from the start of this chapter, but with no formatting.

- Place the cursor anywhere in the first line <u>Styles, Templates and AutoFormat</u>.

- Open the Style box and select **Heading1**.

The pre-defined style is applied to the text to produce a neat heading.

- Move the cursor down to the line with the first subheading <u>Paragraph styles explained</u> (line 4).

- Open the Style box and select **Heading2**.

- Move the cursor down to the line with the next subheading <u>Templates explained</u>.

- Open the Style box and select **Heading2**.

- Finally, move the cursor down to the last subheading <u>AutoFormat.</u>

- Open the Style box and select **Heading2**.

The headings have now been formatted quickly and easily.

- Close the document without saving it.

Using templates

The easiest way to get used to templates is to test those supplied. Many of the templates will start off by asking you for some information - you will have to follow the instructions, make some decisions and click **OK** as and when necessary.

To open a document with a new template, you must use the **File**, **New** menu option. Clicking the **Open** button does not do this.

- Select **File**, **New**.

A list of available templates is displayed. Notice that some of the templates are Wizards. Wizards help you to create documents automatically and are the topic of the next chapter.

- Make sure the Document option is selected.

- Locate and doubleclick the MEMO2 template.

The MEMO2 template produces a new document, much of which has already been done for you. You can now edit this document just like any other document.

- Edit the document according to the picture below and print it out.

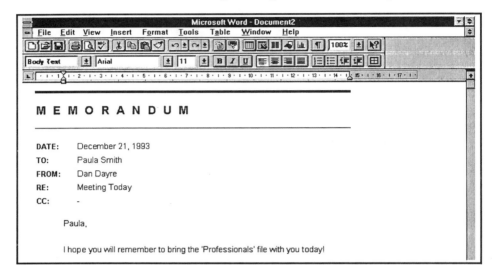

- Close the document without saving the changes.

Experiment

At some point you will want to try out some of the available templates. Open them up and try them out. You can always close the documents you create without saving them.

In conclusion

Using templates and paragraph styles can be a very powerful tool, and very advanced. There are many features that have not been covered in this chapter, specifically about editing paragraph styles and creating new ones. As you grow more confident you will no doubt start experimenting more.

AutoFormat

AutoFormat lets Word have a go at formatting your document for you automatically. You can then accept the suggested formats, or cancel them.

- Close all existing documents.

- Open the file AUTOFORM.DOC from your exercise diskette.

The document has no formatting at the moment.

Using the AutoFormat button

Using the **AutoFormat** button formats the document according to the currently selected format.

- Click the **AutoFormat** button in the toolbar.

Hey presto! your document is automatically formatted. It may not be perfect, but it may have helped a lot.

Undoing AutoFormat

Now undo the changes you just made:

- Select **Edit, Undo AutoFormat**.

Using Format, AutoFormat

Using **AutoFormat** via the menu system offers more flexibility than using the **AutoFormat** button.

- Select **Format, AutoFormat**.

The AutoFormat dialog box is opened.

- Click **OK** to start the formatting.

When it is ready, Word will offer some options in the AutoFormat dialog box. You can accept the formatting or reject it all. You can also review the changes and view the Style Gallery - this allows you to select other AutoFormat styles.

- Click **Style Gallery**.

The Style Gallery dialog box is opened. It shows a preview of your document and a list of templates available.

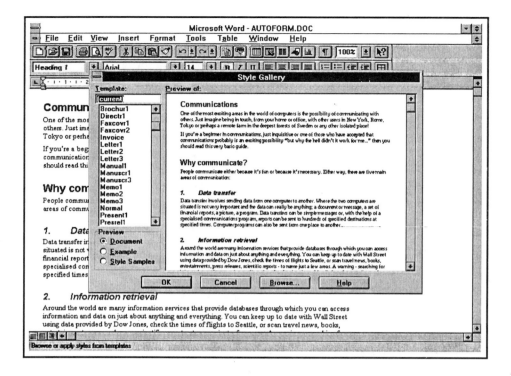

- In the Templates list, select **Manuscr1**.

The new template format is applied and the preview of it is updated.

- In the Templates list, select **Manuscr3**.

- In the Templates list, select **Brochur1**.

Accept this one:

- Click **OK** to confirm the current template.

- Click **Accept** to accept the formatting changes.

You are returned to the main document window and can continue editing and formatting the document as normal.

Ending the session

- Experiment a little with the AutoFormat feature.

- When you are ready, close all documents.

- Exit Word.

Wizards

Wizards are automated templates. By selecting a Wizard, you open a template, as in the previous chapter, but you also get help setting up the document. Word will display dialog boxes and you can fill in necessary details. At the end of the process, the new document is ready for you to edit in the normal manner.

As always, the best way to learn is by example.

The Agenda Wizard

- Start Word, if necessary.

- Select **File**, **New**.

- Doubleclick the **Agenda Wizard** option.

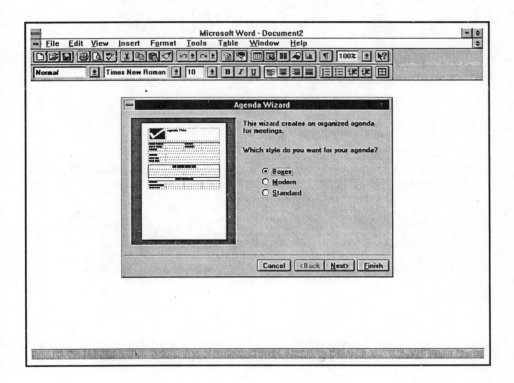

The Agenda Wizard dialog box is opened. Word asks you which style you want for the agenda. At the moment you probably don't know what the styles look like, but the preview box gives you an idea. The **Boxes** option is currently displayed (probably!).

- Click the **Modern** option and check the preview.

- Click the **Standard** option and check the preview.

- Click **Next** to continue.

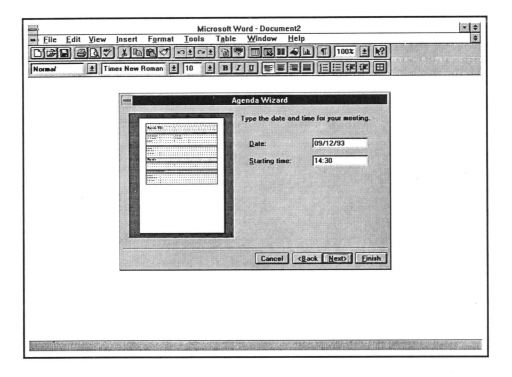

You can use the **Back** button to go back and change the style. Word now asks for details about the date and time of the meeting.

- Doubleclick the Starting Time entry so that it is highlighted.

- Type:

  16:00

- Click **Next** to continue.

Now Word asks for the title and location of the meeting.

- Edit the Title entry so that it reads:

  Weekly Marketing Meeting

- Edit the Location entry so that it reads:

  Conference Room

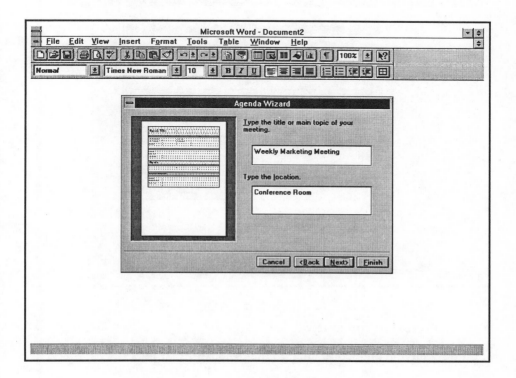

- Click **Next** to continue.

Word asks which headings you want to include.

- Click the **Special notes** option so that it is not crossed.

- Click **Next** to continue.

Word now asks which names you want on the agenda.

- Click the **Facilitator, Observers** and **Resource persons** options so that they are not crossed.

- Click **Next** to continue.

Word now asks you to fill in the agenda topics.

- Fill in the details as in the picture that follows.

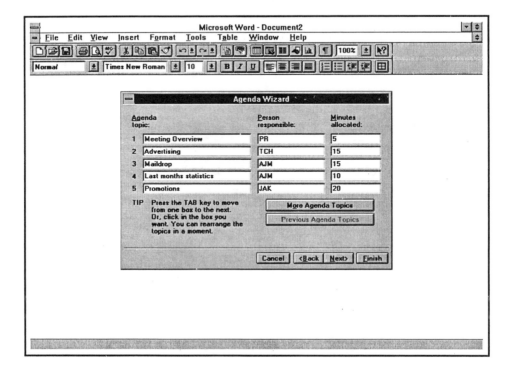

- Click **Next** to continue.

You now have a chance to change the order of the topics.

- Select the fourth topic in the list.

- Click **Move Up** twice to move it up to second place.

- Click **Next** to continue.

The next question is about a form for recording the minutes. **Yes** is already selected and it will be useful to see what the Wizard produces anyway.

- Click **Next** to continue.

The Wizard has now reached the end of its automation process. You can use the **Back** button to go back and change any of the details you have entered, or **Finish** to close the Wizard and get on with the agenda document. There is also an option that will open the Help window.

- Click **Finish** to close the Wizard.

Your agenda document is now created and you can work with it it as a normal document. Notice that the finishing time has automatically been worked out from the amount of time allocated to each topic.

- Print out the document.

- Close the document without saving the changes.

The Fax Wizard

Now try the Fax Wizard out on your own.

- Select **File**, **New**.

- Doubleclick the **FaxWizard** option.

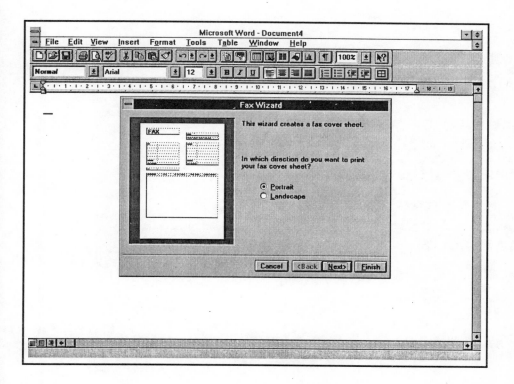

- Run through the questions making appropriate choices.

- When you are ready, click **Finish** to close the Wizard.

The fax document can now be edited in the normal manner. In particular you can add the message and print the fax. Note that the message is added on page 2.

- Close the document without saving the changes.

Ending the session

- Try out another Wizard on your own.

- When you are ready, close the document.

- Exit Word.

AutoCorrect and AutoText

This chapter covers two more useful features that Word provides. Auto-Correct will correct mistakes you make as you type, for example <u>teh</u> can be corrected to <u>the,</u> <u>ENter</u> can be corrected to <u>Enter</u>. AutoText lets you store blocks of text and graphics so that you can quickly recall them and insert them in any document you are working with.

AutoCorrect

AutoCorrect will automatically correct common mistakes you make. However, you need to tell Word which mistakes you often make and provide the correct version. Once you have done this, Word will have learnt your mistakes and will put them right for you.

Word also has a few mistakes already programmed for you.

*   Start off with a fresh document in the Normal view.

*   Select **Tools, AutoCorrect**.

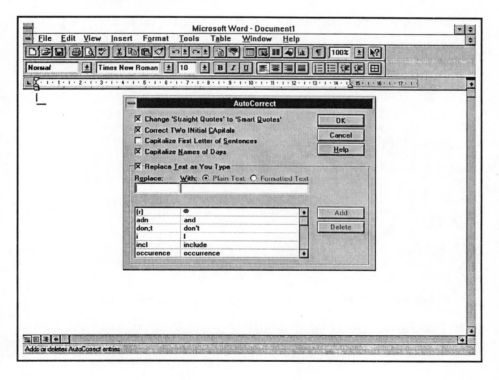

The AutoCorrect dialog box is opened. It has several standard options that you can select and also has a list of personalised corrections that you can add to.

- Click the **Capitalize First Letter of Sentences** option so that it is crossed.

- Inspect the list of corrections, note that the last one is teh to the.

Now try it out:

- Click **OK** to close the AutoCorrect dialog box.

- Type the following paragraph as it stands, and notice how the various mistakes are corrected as you type:

  This morning I woke up in a daze. it was friday night last night and the team had a bit of a do. NAturally i will never do it again, never!

- Press **Enter** twice to conclude the paragraph and create a blank line.

Did you see that? Word automatically changed the it to It, friday to Friday, teh to the, NAturally to Naturally and i to I.

Adding your own corrections

Assume that one of your regular mistakes is that you often type their as thier. Easy, use AutoCorrect to put an end to the mistake.

- Select **Tools, AutoCorrect**.

- In the Replace box, type:

  thier

- In the With box, type:

  their

- Click **Add** to add the correction to the list.

- Click **OK**.

Now try it out:

- Type, with mistakes:

  it's my own fault, after all people are masters of thier own brains!

- Press **Enter** twice to conclude the paragraph and create a blank line.

Yes, Word did the correction for you!

Deleting AutoCorrect corrections

To finish off this section, you will now delete the corrections you have added.

- Select **Tools, AutoCorrect**.

- In the list of corrections, select the **thier** correction and then click **Delete**.

- Click **OK**.

- Close the document without saving it.

AutoText

AutoText gives you the ability to store often used phrases and graphics so that you can recall them quickly at any time. For example you could shorten the company name <u>XYZ Press (UK) Limited</u> to just <u>XYZ</u>. This was called the Glossary in Word for Windows v2.

 The AutoText button on the toolbar has two uses and the its name switches between **Edit AutoText** (when text is selected and Word assumes you are planning to save an AutoText entry) and **Insert AutoText** (when no text is selected and Word assumes you are about to insert an AutoText entry in your document).

- Click the **New** button on the toolbar to open a new document.

Let's assume that you often use the phrase "Further to our telephone conversation today,". You can use AutoText to store the phrase. You will also store the XYZ company name mentioned above.

- Type:

  Further to our telephone conversation today,

- Select the complete phrase.

- Select **Edit, AutoText,** or click the **Edit AutoText** button on the toolbar.

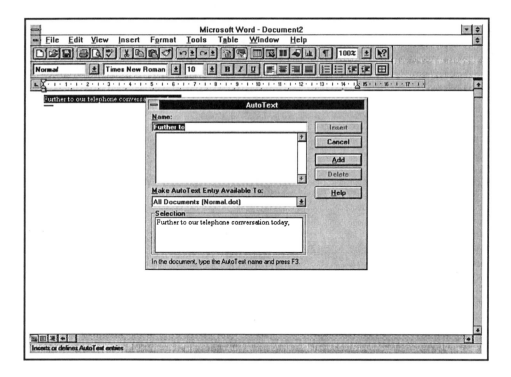

The AutoText dialog box is opened. Each entry is given a name and the
The name box already suggests the name **Further to**. In the Selection box,
you will see the selected text.

- Click **Add** to add the phrase to the AutoText list.

You are returned to the document.

- Delete the phrase starting Further to.

- Type:

  XYZ Press (UK) Limited

- Select the complete company name.

- Select **Edit**, **AutoText**, or click the **Edit AutoText** button on the
  toolbar.

You don't have to accept the AutoText name that Word suggests. In this
case it would be appropriate to give it the name XYZ.

- Edit the AutoText name to **XYZ** (see picture on next page).

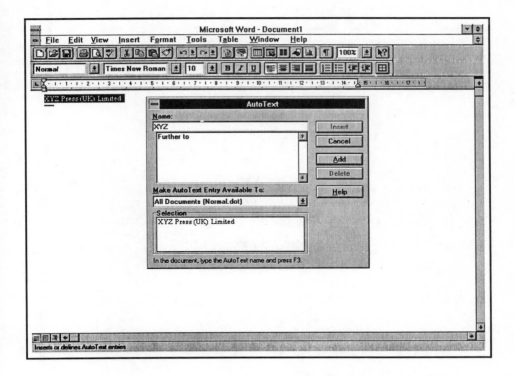

- Click **Add** to add the phrase to the AutoText list.

You are returned to the document.

Trying AutoText out

When you use AutoText to insert text into your document, you can use the **Edit**, **AutoText** menu option. This will display a list of AutoText entries available from which you can select the desired one. In the exercise that follows, however, you will learn the automatic function of this feature.

- Start off by deleting the current text so that you have an empty document.

- Press **Enter** 3 times.

- Type the following:

  **Mr P Squires
  14 West End
  DURSLEY
  Glos
  GL0 0AA**

- Press **Enter** 3 times.

Now add the date:

- Select **Insert, Date and Time**.

- Doubleclick one of the date options in the list.

- Press **Enter** 3 times.

- Type:

  Dear Mr Squires,

- Press **Enter** twice.

Now use AutoText to insert your phrase:

- Type:

  Further to

- Click the **Insert AutoText** button on the toolbar.

The phrase is now completed automatically.

- Type, starting with a space:

  I am enclosing a replacement diskette. XYZ

- Click the **Insert AutoText** button on the toolbar again.

The company name is now completed automatically.

- Type:

  is sorry for any inconvenience caused.

  Yours sincerely,

  M. Appleton.

- Print the letter if you so wish.

It is easy to see how you could quickly build up a set of phrases and be able to quickly create standard letters with varying content.

Deleting AutoText entries

Finish off now by deleting the AutoText entry you added.

- Select **Edit, AutoText**.
- Select the **Further to** entry.
- Click **Delete**.

The phrase is now deleted from the AutoText list.

- Select the **XYZ** entry.
- Click **Delete**.

The name is now deleted from the AutoText list.

- Click **Close** to close the dialog box.

Ending the session

- Experiment by adding a new phrase, testing it and then deleting it.
- When you are ready, close the document without saving it.
- Exit Word.

Undo and Redo

No one can accuse Microsoft of under-providing when it comes to Word's ability to undo changes you make to your document. Word keeps track of the 100 last changes you made and you can undo any of them individually. Not satisfied with that, you can also undo your undos, otherwise known as redo.

- Open the file COSTA.DOC from your exercise diskette.

Using Edit Undo

Apart from the Undo and Redo feature that will be covered next, Word has an **Undo** option in the **Edit** menu. This can be used to quickly undo the last operation. The menu option actually changes to mirror what you did, so the Undo option could read **Undo Bold**, **Undo Clear**, etc.

- Select the whole of the title <u>The Costa del Fortune</u>.
- Click the **Bold** button on the toolbar.
- Click anywhere on the text to remove the selection highlight.
- Open the **Edit** menu and click **Undo Bold**.
- Click anywhere on the text to remove the selection highlight.

The bold feature is undone.

- Select the word **del** in the title.
- Click **Delete** to delete the word.
- Open the **Edit** menu and click **Undo Clear**.
- Click anywhere on the text to remove the selection highlight.

The deletion is undone and the word replaced in the document.

Undo and Redo

The Undo and Redo features allow you to undo and redo multiple changes.

☞ *There are a few changes, such as printing and saving documents, that you cannot undo.*

- Position the cursor anywhere in the second paragraph.
- Click the **Center** button.
- Select the whole of the second paragraph and drag it down after the third paragraph.
- Select the whole of the first paragraph and press **Delete** to delete it.

Now try undoing some of the changes:

- Click the **Undo** button on the toolbar to open the list of changes.

☞ *In some versions of Word there is a bug and the program may lock up at this point - if it does, you will have to re-start your computer.*

- Select one of the changes and see it undone.
- repeat the Undo process with a different change.

Now try redoing one of the undone changes:

- Click the **Redo** button on the toolbar to open the list of undone changes.
- Select one of the undone changes in the list and see it re-done.

Ending the session

- Experiment a little more with Undo and Redo.
- When you are ready, close the document without saving the changes.
- Exit Word.

Borders

Word provides an attractive feature that allows you to put a border round a paragraph. You can also add some background shading.

- Open the document HEART.DOC from your exercise diskette.

Paragraph borders

A paragraph can be attractively emphasised by boxing it in.

- Position the cursor anywhere in the paragraph that starts <u>This term measures</u>...).

- Select **Format**, **Borders and Shading.**

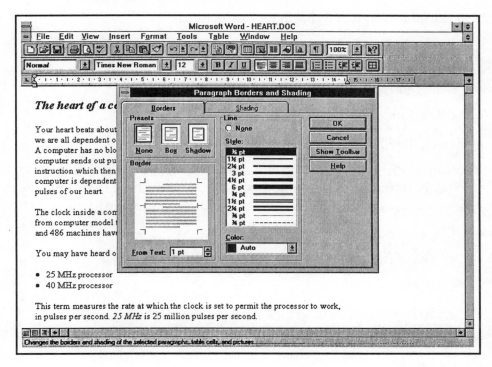

The Paragraph Borders and Shading dialog box is opened and has two file cards, one for Borders, which is displayed now, and one for Shading.

The three preset types allow you to quickly select no border, a simple box border and a box border with a shadow behind it. You can also select a line thickness and a colour for the border.

- Click the Preset option **Shadow**.

Your choice is previewed in the Border box.

- Click **OK**.

The paragraph is now boxed. It may look better slightly indented as well.

- Select **Format, Paragraph**.

- Enter a value of **0.5"** (or **1 cm**) in the left and right indent boxes.

- Click **OK**.

Shading

You can add background shading to any paragraph.

- Select the list of five bulleted paragraphs starting with <u>8088 (Used in plain PC and XT machines)</u>.

- Select **Format, Borders and Shading**.

- Click the Box option in the from the Preset types.

- Click the **Shading** tab.

You can set the amount of shading and the foreground and background colours. If you are not using a colour printer, you will have to try out how various percentage shadings and background colours look when printed.

- Click the **5%** shading option.

- Click the Background option and select **Yellow**.

- Click **OK**.

- Print the document, or use the Print Preview feature, to see the effects of the borders and shading you have added.

Experiment!

- Experiment with some of the other paragraphs. Finish off by closing the document.

Graphics and Frames

You can import graphics images that you have created with other programs into your Word document. In this chapter, you will first learn to import graphics using the **Insert, Picture** option. The inserted picture is treated like a single character in the document and will move around as text is added or deleted.

You will also learn about inserting frames which are independent of the text around them.

You can use the following file types in Word:

Program	*Filename extension*
Windows Bitmaps	.bmp
Windows Metafile	.wmf
Draw Perfect	.wpg
Micrografx Designer/Draw	.drw
AutoCad	.dxf
HP Graphic Language	.hgl
Computer Graphics Metafile	.cgm
Encapsulated PostScript	.eps
Tagged Image Format	.tif
PC Paintbrush	.pcx
Lotus 1-2-3 Graphic	.pic
AutoCad Pilot File	.plt

In this chapter, you will open the file LASER.DOC from your exercise diskette and add a picture LASER.PCX to it.

- Open the file LASER.DOC from your exercise diskette.

- If it is not already selected, select the **Page Layout** view.

Inserting a PCX picture file

The next stage is to insert the PCX picture. As mentioned, a picture is treated as a single character and will move as you add or delete text. You should, therefore, position the cursor before importing the picture.

- Position the cursor on the empty line between the first and second paragraphs.

- Select **Insert**, **Picture**.

- Open the Drives box and select **a:**.

- In the list of files, locate and doubleclick the filename **laser.pcx**.

The picture is inserted in the document at the cursors position.

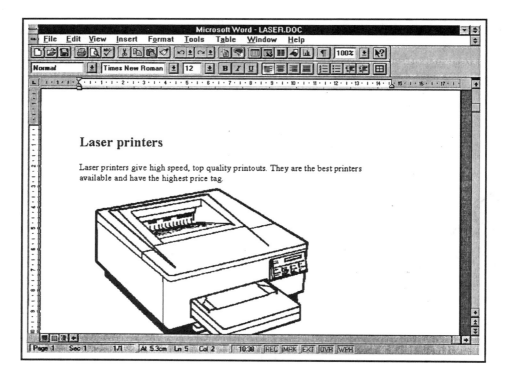

Re-sizing the picture

A picture can be re-sized to make it smaller or larger. Clicking on the picture produces *frame handles*, small squares around the picture frame, which are used to increase or decrease the size of the picture.

- Click anywhere on the picture.

The frame handles appear.

- Position the mouse pointer over the bottom right-hand corner frame handle - you may need to scroll the document downwards to do this - the mouse pointer will become a double-headed diagonal arrow.

When you now drag the frame handle about to alter the picture size, the Scaling changes you are making are shown in the Status bar, bottom left-hand corner of the screen, in percentages. Keep an eye on them as you proceed.

☞ *If you want to keep the picture with the same proportions as the original size, the High and Wide scaling percentages should be equal.*

- Hold down the mouse button and drag the frame handle inwards and upwards to reduce the picture until the Scaling is shown as about 55% High and 55% Wide, then release the mouse button.

The picture should now be reduced (see picture on next page).

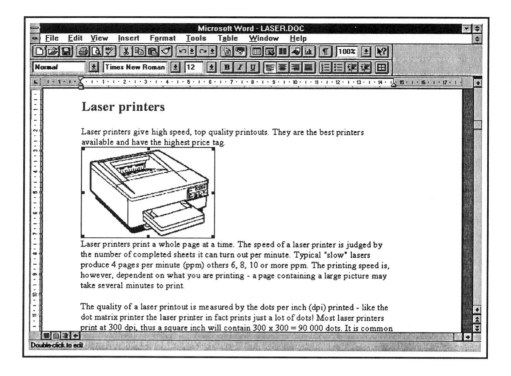

Remember a picture is treated as a single character, so try centring it:

- With the picture still selected, click the **Center** button in the toolbar.

The picture is now centred, but could do with a little more space above and below it.

- Position the cursor at the very end of the first paragraph.

- Press **Enter**.

- Position the cursor at the very beginning of the second paragraph.

- Press **Enter**.

Use Print Preview

- To see the page better, select **Print Preview**.

- When you are ready, click **Close**.

Deleting a picture

Deleting a picture is very simple. Suppose you don't want the picture in your document:

- Click anywhere on the picture so that it is selected.

- Press the **Delete** key.

The picture is deleted.

- Now close the document without saving the changes.

Creating independent frames

By creating a frame, which can then be filled with text, a picture, a graph, etc., the frame is independent of its position in the document. It can be moved around and the text can flow round it.

- Open the file MATRIX.DOC from your exercise diskette.

- Select **Insert, Frame**.

- If necessary, confirm that you want to switch to the Page Layout view.

As you move the mouse pointer over the text now, it appears as a small cross.

- Before proceeding, check the picture on the next page to see what you are trying to achieve.

- Position the mouse pointer between the first and second paragraphs.

- Hold the mouse button down and drag out a frame to roughly the same size as in the picture on the next page.

The frame is ready. Notice how the text wraps around the frame.

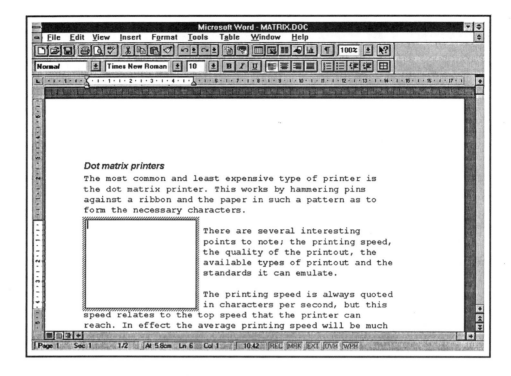

Inserting the picture

Now fill the frame with a picture:

- Make sure the frame is selected - the frame will be surrounded by small diagonal lines and the cursor will be blinking inside it.

- Select **Insert, Picture**.

- If necessary, open the Drives box and select **a:**.

- In the list of files, locate and doubleclick the filename **matrix.pcx**.

The picture is inserted into the frame.

Dragging a frame

It is very easy to move a frame. Simply select the frame by clicking on it, and the drag it to its new position.

- Select the frame.

- Drag it over to the right-hand side of the page.

- To see the page better, select **Print Preview**.

- When you are ready, click **Close**.

Experiment

- Now try experimenting with the document, picture and frame.

- When you are ready, close the document.

Clip art

Word comes supplied with a selection of ready made clip art pictures to be found in the C:\WINWORD\CLIPART directory. They are stored as Windows Metafile files with a **.WMF** file extension. You will now try using some of these.

- Open a new document.

- Select **Insert**, **Picture**.

- In the Drives list, select **c:**.

- In the Directories list, locate and doubleclick the **clipart** directory (it is a subdirectory of WINWORD, so click **c:**, then find and click **winword**, then **clipart**).

Previewing a picture

To help you choose a picture, you can preview any picture in the list.

- If necessary, click the **Preview Picture** option so that it is crossed.

Any selected files will now be shown in the Preview box.

- Locate and click the <u>anchor.wmf</u> filename.

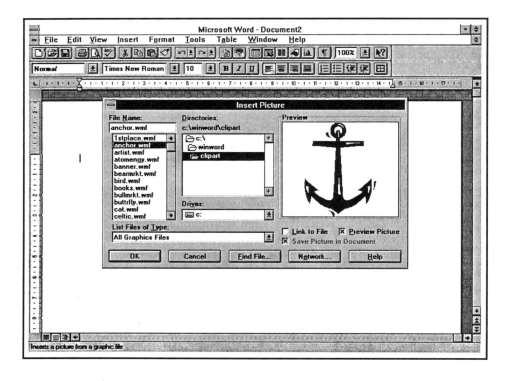

- Select other pictures and preview them.

- Finally, doubleclick the <u>anchor.wmf</u> filename.

The picture is inserted in your document, at the cursor's position, and you can add some text to it. If the picture is not displayed, then use the **Print Preview** feature to inspect it.

Cropping and scaling a picture

Cropping a picture means trimming it. You can trim any edge by any amount. You can also scale it, or choose an exact size.

- Select the anchor picture by clicking anywhere on it.

- Select **Format, Picture**.

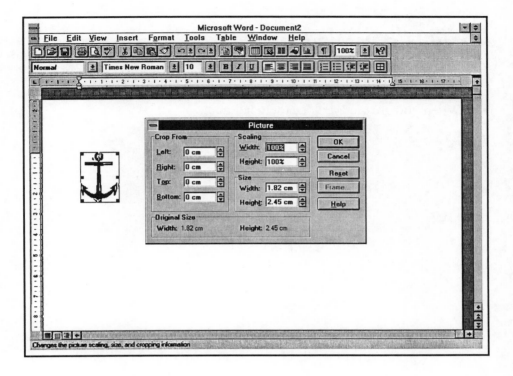

- Now try cropping the picture yourself by entering different values and checking the result. Then try different scaling percentages. Click **OK** for each change to inspect the result.

- When you are ready, use the **Reset** button to restore the picture to its original size.

Deleting frames

To delete a frame, or picture, select it, then press the **Delete** key.

- Select the anchor picture by clicking on it.

- Press the **Delete** key.

Undoing a deletion

If you really did not mean to delete the picture, you can undo your deletion via the **Edit**, **Undo** option.

Ending the session.

- Experiment some more on your own with pictures and frames, in particular try inserting a frame and and adding text to the frame.

- When you are ready, close the document.

- Exit Word.

Mail Merge

Using the **Mail Merge** function in Word, you can create standard letters, and link them to data files for mass mailing - for example, a newsletter and an address list.

The standard procedure is as follows:

☺ Create a main document that has the fixed text.

☺ Create a data document that contains the variable, or data, text.

☺ Print the documents using Mail Merge.

For this exercise, you will create a letter and mailing list and then merge them.

Creating the main document

The main document is a standard document, just like all the others you have been writing in this course.

- Make sure you are starting off with a fresh document in the Normal view.

- Open the Font Size list on the toolbar and select **12**.

- Type, with suitable empty lines:

Dear

Thank you very much for your enquiry about our range of products. Please find enclosed our catalogue and current price list. I would like to point out that the sale ends on 31st May 1994.

Yours sincerely,

P Squires
For and on behalf of XYZ Ltd.

Now save the document:

- Make sure your exercise diskette is in drive A.

- Select **File**, **Save**, or
  click the **Save** button on the toolbar, or
  press **Ctrl+S**.

- In the File Name box, type:

  a:letter

- Press **Enter** or click **OK**.

The document will need adjusting to allow for the merge fields. You will do this later. For the time being, close the document.

- Select **File**, **Close**.

Creating a data document

The next stage is to create a data document. The first line of the data document should list the field names. Use the Table feature to do this.

- Open a new document.

- Click the **Insert Table** button in the toolbar, and select a table 11x7.

You should now have an empty table.

- Type in the table headings as follows:

  title initials surname address1 address2 town postcode

- Now fill in the table with the names and addresses shown on the next page.

☞ *Do not use commas and full stops within an address, for example after the number of the street, as this may cause problems for you at a later date if you wish to 'export' your data to another program.*

☞ *Don't worry if any entry does not fit in on one line, this will not affect the actual data itself. Another time, you could also adjust the widths of the columns if you wish.*

title	init's	surname	address1	address2	town	postcode
Mr	K	Wilkes	4 The Tyhe	Middleton	STROUD	GL33 7QW
Mr	T T	Davies	25 Queens St	Brockford	GLOUCESTER	GL0 9RT
Dr	F D	Rodmoor	Sunnyside	Main Road	DURSLEY	GL4 4QQ
Ms	E W	Quincy	33 High St		READING	RG1 2WW
Ms	A	Halliwell	2 Stroud Rd	Halisbury	OXFORD	OX23 6FG
Ms	H D	Knight	The Gays	Melbury	SWINDON	SN1 7AP
Mr	P	Farthing	1 William St	Pilbury	BRISTOL	BS12 6BS
Prof	D J	Breech	44 Arms Drive	Gleebury	BATH	BA1 9QC
Ms	R	Samson	18 The Avenue		CARDIFF	CF3 2PL
Mr	W	Whipp	Hope House	Mile End	LONDON	W3Q 1WW

Your screen should resemble the following picture:

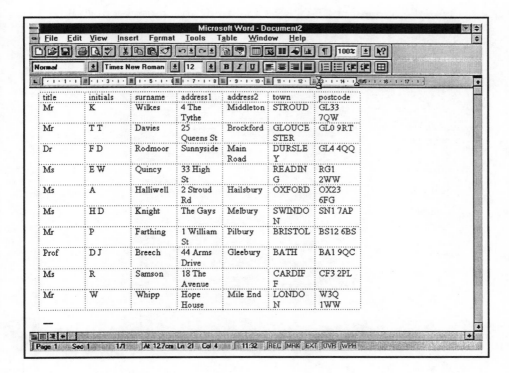

When you are ready, save the document:

- Make sure your exercise diskette is in drive A.

- Select **File**, **Save**, or
  click the **Save** button on the toolbar, or
  press **Ctrl+S**.

- In the File Name box, type:

  a:address

- Press **Enter** or click **OK**.

For the time being, close the document.

- Select **File, Close**.

Setting up the mail merge

It is now time to merge the two documents.

- Open the document LETTER.DOC from your exercise diskette.

- Select **Tools, Mail Merge**.

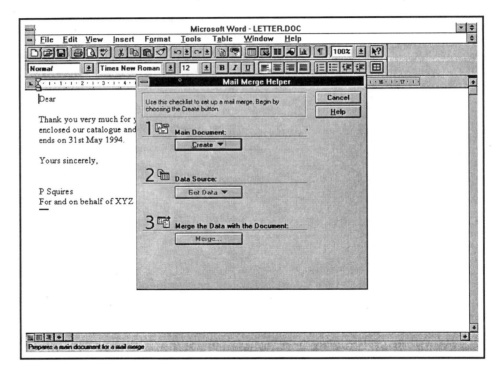

The Mail Merge Helper dialog box is displayed. The first stage is to create or select the main document.

- Click **Create** and select **Form Letters**.

Word gives you the option of using the currently active document as the main document, or creating a new one.

- Click **Active Window**.

A new **Edit** button is added to the dialog box. Stage 2 is to select the data source. Again this can be an existing data file, or you can create a new one.

- Click **Get Data** and select **Open Data Source**.

The Open Data Source dialog box is displayed and resembles the standard Open dialog box.

- In the File Name box, type:

  a:address

- Press **Enter** or click **OK**.

Adding data fields to the main document

At this point, Word checks the main document and finds that there aren't any merge fields in it. These merge fields are used to insert the information for each letter taken from the data document.

- Click **Edit Main Document**.

You are returned to the main document and can add some merge fields. Start off by adding some empty lines at the top.

- Make sure the cursor is at the top of the document (**Ctrl+Home**).

- Press **Enter** 5 times, then move the cursor up 2 lines.

Now add the name and address fields. This is done by using the **Insert Merge Field** button on the Mail Merge toolbar that was automatically added to the display. Each selected merge field is added to the main document at the current cursor position.

- Click the **Insert Merge Field** button.

A list of available fields is shown.

- Click the **title** field.

<<title>> is added to the main document.

- Press the **Spacebar** to insert a blank space.

- Click the **Insert Merge Field** button again.

- Click the **initials** entry.

- Press **Spacebar** to insert a blank space.

- Click the **Insert Merge Field** button again.

- Click the **surname** entry.

- Press **Enter** to move the cursor down to the next line.

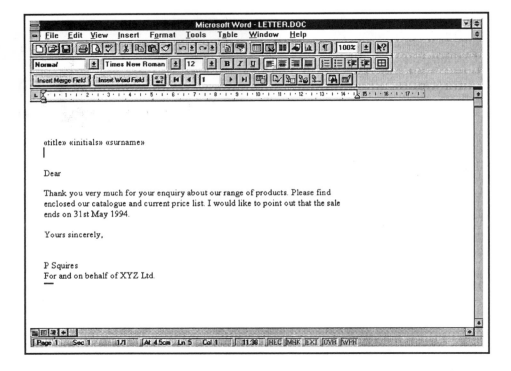

- Click the **Insert Merge Field** button again.

- Click **address1**.

- Press **Enter** to move the cursor down to the next line.

- Click the **Insert Merge Field** button again.

- Click **address2**.

- Press **Enter** to move the cursor down to the next line.

- Click the **Insert Merge Field** button again.

- Click **town**.

- Press **Enter** to move the cursor down to the next line.

- Click the **Insert Merge Field** button again.

- Click **postcode**.

- Press **Enter** 3 times to create some empty lines.

Finally, you need to insert the name in the salutation.

- Move the cursor to just after the salutation <u>Dear</u> .

- Press the **Spacebar** to insert a blank space.

- Click the **Insert Merge Field** button again.

- Click **title**.

- Press **Spacebar** to insert a blank space.

- Click the **Insert Merge Field** button again.

- Click **surname**.

- Type a comma (,).

Adding the date

As a final touch, you can add a date field. The advantage of doing this with a field, rather than typing in a date, is that the date is always adjusted to the date of the printout.

- Move the cursor up to a blank line before the salutation.

- Select **Insert, Date and Time**.

- Select the date format of your choice by doubleclicking it.

The date is now inserted.

- Finish off by tidying up the document adding empty lines where necessary.

- As a good measure, save your document (**Ctrl+S**).

Merging the documents

Now the big test!

- Select **Tools**, **Mail Merge**.

- Click **Merge**.

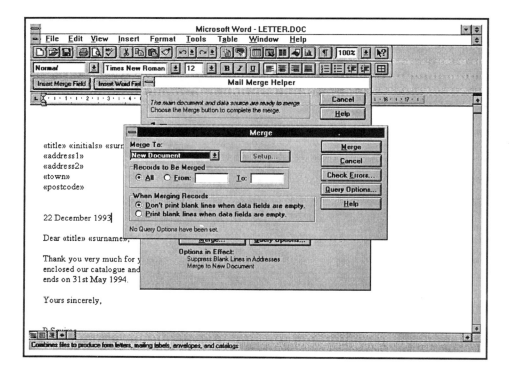

Various options are presented, but you can just accept the default settings now. In particular, the Merge To options lets you merge to a file, to a printer, or to electronic mail.

- Make sure the **New Document** option is selected in the Merge To box.

- Click **Merge** to start the merge.

After a while, a new document window is opened containing a copy of all the letters. The file can be printed in the normal manner.

- Close the current document window without saving the changes.

Merge and print

Now repeat the merge process, but print the documents instead, but only pages 1 to 3 to save paper!

- Select **Tools**, **Mail Merge**.

- Click **Merge**.

- Open the Merge To box and select **Printer**.

- Click the **From** option and fill in **1** To **3**.

- Click **Merge** to start the merge.

The three letters are printed. All you need to do now is scan a copy of your signature so that it is saved as a picture on your hard disk, then add the picture to the main document!

Ending the session

- When you are ready, close any open documents without saving the changes.

- Exit Word.

Mail Merge

Addressing Envelopes and Mailing Labels

Word for Windows provides an easy method of addressing envelopes and labels and you can also use Mail Merge to print a set of mailing labels.

Addressing envelopes

When addressing an envelope, you can simply type in the name and address, or if it already exists in your document, Word can automatically extract it for you.

- Open the ENV.DOC file from your exercise diskette and switch to the Normal view.

- Select the whole of the address at the top of the letter.

- Open the **Tools** menu and select **Envelopes and Labels**.

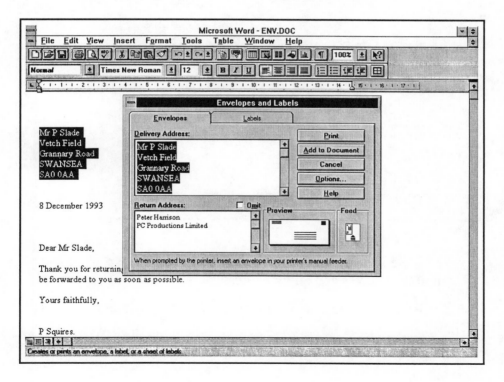

The Envelopes and Labels dialog box is opened. Notice that Word has automatically filled in the address for you. There is also a box for the return address.

- Make sure the **Envelopes** options are shown.

Options

When setting up an address for an envelope, there are two options that need to be looked at, Envelope options and Printing options. The instructions that follow will act as a guide only, you may have to set the options to suit your own stationery and printer.

- Click the **Options** button.

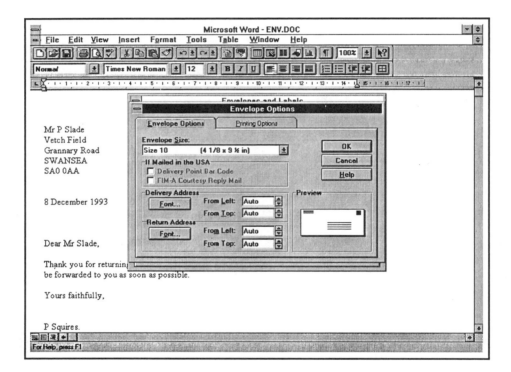

⊕ The Envelope Options allow you to choose an envelope type and position the address and return address.

⊕ The Printing Options allow you to set how the envelope is to be fed in.

- Make any changes necessary to suit your system, then click **OK**.

- Edit the Delivery Address and the Return Address, if needed.

- Click **Print** to print the envelope or **Cancel** to close the dialog box without printing.

Labels

Labels can be printed in exactly the same way.

- Select the whole of the address at the top of the letter.

Open the **Tools** menu and select **Envelopes and Labels**.

- Click the **Labels** tab.

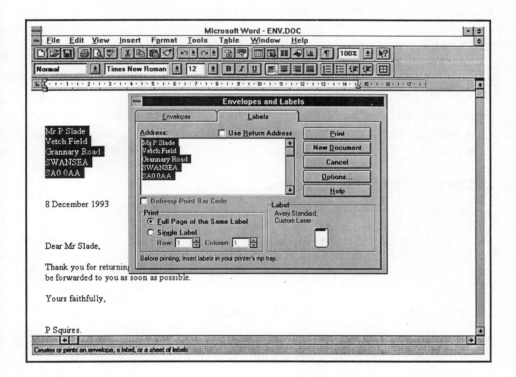

Options

Once again there are some options available.

- Click the **Options** button.

⊕ The Label Options allow you to choose a label type, or to set up a custom label. The measurement details for a custom label can be changed by clicking the **Details** button.

- Make any changes necessary to suit your labels, then click **OK**.

- Edit the Delivery Address, if needed.

- Click **Print** to print the envelope or **Cancel** to close the dialog box without printing.

- Close the document without saving the changes.

Printing mailing labels

Printing mailing labels involves merging a main document with a data document, as discussed in the previous chapter. In this exercise, you will print out the addresses contained in the ADDRESS.DOC data file on your exercise diskette. If you do not have any labels, you can still follow the exercise up to the point of the actual printout.

Setting up the main document

- Click the **New** button to open a new document.

- Select **Tools, Mail Merge**.

The Mail Merge Helper dialog box is displayed. The first stage is to create or select the main document.

- Click **Create** and select **Mailing Labels**.

Word gives you the option of using the currently active document as the main document, or creating a new one.

- Click **Active Window**.

A new **Edit** button is added to the dialog box allowing you to change the main document.

Now select the data source. Again this can be an existing data file, or you can create a new one.

- Click **Get Data** and select **Open Data Source**.

The Open Data Source dialog box is displayed and resembles the standard Open dialog box.

- In the File Name box, type:

  a:address

- Press **Enter** or click **OK**.

Setting up the main document

At this point, Word checks the main document and finds that there aren't any merge fields in it. These merge fields are used to insert the information for each label taken from the data document.

- Click **Set Up Main Document**.

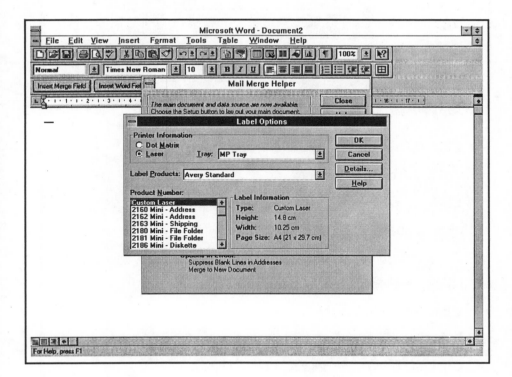

The Label Options dialog box is opened and you can select a label type.

- Use the **Printer Information, Label Products** and **Product Number** options to select your printer and label details, then click **OK**.

The Create Labels dialog box is opened for you to add the address fields.

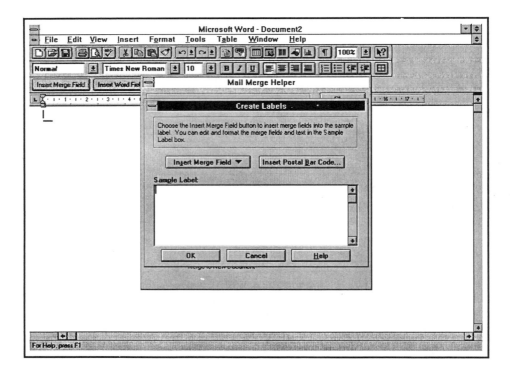

- Click the **Insert Merge Field** button.

A list of available fields is shown.

- Click the **title** field.

<<title>> is added to the main document.

- Press the **Spacebar** to insert a blank space.

- Click the **Insert Merge Field** button again.

- Click the **initials** entry.

- Press **Spacebar** to insert a blank space.

- Click the **Insert Merge Field** button again.

- Click the **surname** entry.
- Press **Enter** to move the cursor down to the next line.
- Click the **Insert Merge Field** button again.
- Click **address1**.
- Press **Enter** to move the cursor down to the next line.
- Click the **Insert Merge Field** button again.
- Click **address2**.
- Press **Enter** to move the cursor down to the next line.
- Click the **Insert Merge Field** button again.
- Click **town**.
- Press **Enter** to move the cursor down to the next line.
- Click the **Insert Merge Field** button again.
- Click **postcode**.

Your label is now ready.

- Click **OK**.

You are returned to the Mail Merge Helper dialog box.

- Click **Merge**.

The Merge dialog box is displayed.

- In the Merge To: box, select **New Document** or **Printer**, as required.
- Click **Merge**.

After a short time, the labels are printed, or displayed in a document.

Ending the session

- Finish off by closing all the open documents without saving the changes.
- Exit Word.

Sorting

Once you have created a number of lists and documents, you will sometimes need to sort them in a specific order - alphabetically or numerically.
This can be achieved by using the **Table**, **Sort** feature.

Sorting a table

You can sort a table by selecting the whole table, or a specific column in
the table. If you select the whole table, it will be sorted according to the
contents of the first column. If you select a column, you can mark just part
of the column if you want to sort just that section of the table.

- Open the SORT.DOC file from your exercise diskette.

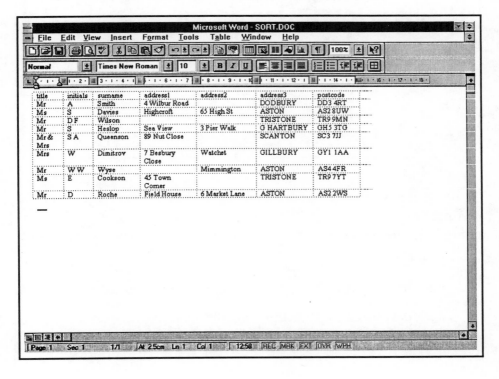

title	initials	surname	address1	address2	address3	postcode
Mr	A	Smith	4 Wilbur Road		DODBURY	DD3 4RT
Ms	S	Davies	Highcroft	65 High St	ASTON	AS2 8UW
Mr	D F	Wilson			TRISTONE	TR9 9MN
Mr	S	Heslop	Sea View	3 Pier Walk	G HARTBURY	GH5 3TG
Mr & Mrs	S A	Queenson	89 Nut Close		SCANTON	SC3 7JJ
Mrs	W	Dimitrov	7 Besbury Close	Watchet	GILLBURY	GY1 1AA
Mr	W W	Wyse		Mimmington	ASTON	AS4 4FR
Ms	E	Cookson	45 Town Corner		TRISTONE	TR9 7YT
Mr	D	Roche	Field House	6 Market Lane	ASTON	AS2 2WS

30-1

- Select the third column containing the surnames, but excluding the title row, from Smith to Roche.

- Select **Table**, **Sort**.

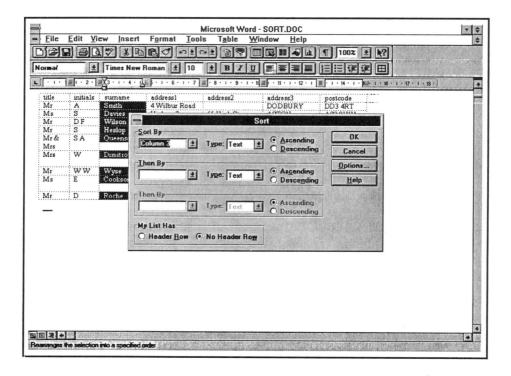

The Sort dialog box is opened allowing you to change the column for sorting, the type of sort and the order. Notice that there is a My List Has option allowing you to say if your selection includes a header row or not.

- Click **OK**.

The table should now be in alphabetical order, according to the surnames.

- Close the document without saving the changes.

Sort options

Each time you select Sort, you can make four settings to control the sort.

Text/Number/Date

You should select Number if you are sorting a column of numbers. This will make sure that any spaces or differences of alignment with decimal points do not interfere with the correct sorting of your column. On any other occasion you would use the Text option.

Ascending/Descending

The normal Ascending sequence for a sort is as follows:

- ☺ Punctuation marks come first, followed by numbers then letters.

- ☺ Upper-case letters come before lower-case if you choose to distinguish between them using the case option.

A Descending sort reverses the order.

Options - Case Sensitive

If you select this option, upper-case letters will be separated out from lower-case during the sort (e.g. Albert, Zachariah, ethelred, porcupine).

Options - Sort Column Only

If you select this option, only the actual cells that are selected will be repositioned. In most cases however, you will want all the information in one row to be kept together even if you are sorting by one of the columns. You would normally, therefore, not select this option.

Sorting paragraphs

It is just as easy to sort paragraphs.

- Load the document TECHTERM.DOC from your exercise diskette.

Study the document to see that the paragraphs are not sorted.

- Select the whole text (**Ctrl+A**).

- Select **Table, Sort Text**.

The Sort Text dialog box is opened with the same options. Just accept the settings as they are.

- Click **OK**.

The document is sorted, rearranging the paragraphs in alphabetical order.

Ending the session

You have now completed this chapter.

- When you are ready, close the document without saving the changes.

- Exit Word.

What is Windows?

In plain English, Windows lets you control and interact with your computer by pointing at symbols (called *icons*) and selecting from menus rather than having to remember the assorted DOS commands. Technically speaking, it is called a *Graphical User Interface* or GUI.

Windows also enables you to have several different programs running at the same time by starting different programs in different windows. This can be a great advantage if you often need to refer to the files in one program (a database or spreadsheet, for instance) while using another program, since you do not have to exit each program every time you swap.

There are also a number of useful accessories provided in your Windows package, including a clock, calculator, diary, drawing program and word-processor.

Windows is not a program in the normal sense of the word, like a word processor or a spreadsheet. It is a complete system, or shell, rather like DOS itself, that allows you to manage disks, documents, programs, etc. in its own way - the way that you will learn by following this course.

The advantages of Windows

The two main advantages of Windows are:

☺ Programs that are written especially for Windows have many common features. Once you have learned to operate Windows itself, or a Windows program, you will have learned how to operate all programs written for Windows.

☺ A few individuals will find it most useful to be able to run several programs at one time and be able to extract information (text or a picture) from one program and insert it into another one.

The main disadvantage is:

☺ By its very nature, Windows needs a fast computer with lots of memory if you are to be able to work quickly and effectively. You may be presented with the Insufficient memory message, i.e. the computer needs more resources. A 25 MHz 386SX computer with at least 2 Mb RAM is the minimum specification, but 4 Mb RAM is preferable, unless you are prepared to accept a slow down at times.

The Windows screen

Below is a picture of a typical Windows screen, with the individual parts labelled. Don't try to learn all these names now, you will pick them up quickly enough when you are using them.. Refer back to this picture as and when you need to.

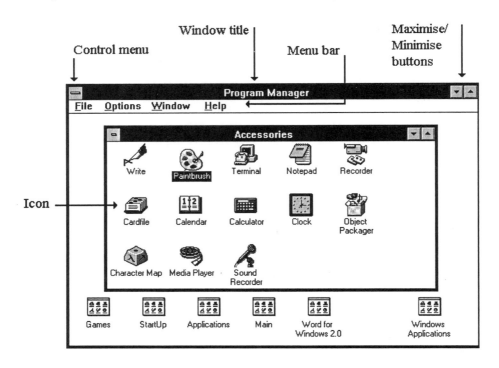

Icons and the mouse pointer

An icon is a picture that represents some kind of object - it might be a program or group of programs - that you want to use or alter in some way.

The mouse pointer is moved by the mouse, and is used to select an item that you want, whether it is a menu, an icon, a file, a window, etc. When the computer is busy, for example writing a file to disk, the pointer will change to an hourglass ($\mathbb{Z}$).

Operating Windows functions

In principle, there are two basic methods of working with Windows functions - using a mouse or using the keyboard.

You will probably find that a combination of mouse and keyboard provide the most efficient way of using Windows. It is possible to get by using just the keyboard or just the mouse, but you may find this a little slow or tedious. In this course you will learn to use both the mouse and keyboard as appropriate for the various commands.

Using the mouse

Using the mouse is clearly the easiest way to use Windows in general. You can quickly move the cursor around, open windows, open menus and make selections. There are four essential mouse operations; point, click, double-click and drag.

Operation	Description
Point	To point using the mouse, simply move your mouse across your desk or mouse mat (or roll your trackball). The pointer on the screen will follow your movement. To point to a particular item, a menu or icon for instance, move your mouse so that the pointer is over the desired object.
Click	To click means that you should press the LEFT mouse button ONCE. As a rule, Windows always uses the left mouse button, although some of the programs you may run under Windows will use both.
Doubleclick	Press the left mouse button TWICE in quick succession. If you do this too slowly, your computer will interpret this as two single clicks. It is possible to set how quickly you need to doubleclick using the Control Panel. This is explained later in the course.
Drag	First position the pointer over an object, press the left mouse button down and hold it down while you move the mouse. The object will be dragged around until you release the mouse button.

These four simple actions, coupled with the occasional use of the keyboard, will allow you to control Windows.

☞ *It is possible to set up the mouse for left-handed people so that the left and right-hand button functions are swapped. This course makes no allowance for such a change, so if you change the mouse you will also have to think about clicking the right-hand button instead of the left-hand button, and vice versa.*

Using the keyboard

All of Windows features can be accessed using the keyboard. Instead of pointing and clicking on menus and selection boxes, for example, you can select features by pressing the right keys. To open the **File** menu, for example, you would press **Alt+F**.

Short cut keys

Some of the most important features have what is known as short cut keys. For example, if you have several windows open at the same time, you could press **Alt+Tab** to swap between the Windows. Some of these short cut keys are very useful, as you will find out.

Starting Windows

- Switch on your computer and printer.

If your computer has a menu system installed, with Windows as one of the menu options, start Windows by selecting that option in the normal way.

Otherwise, when the system prompt (C:>) appears, proceed as follows:

- Type:

  win

- Press the **Enter** key.

☞ *It is possible to set up your computer so that it automatically starts Windows each time you start your computer. To do this, you need to adjust the file called AUTOEXEC.BAT to include the command **win** at the end. It may be advisable to seek the help of an experienced user to do this.*

Windows will display a start up screen for a few seconds.

Program Manager

Whenever you start Windows it will always automatically start the program called **Program Manager**. This program gives you overall control of the Windows system, and it is from here that you can start to work with other applications.

☞ *It is important to note that the picture above and subsequent pictures, may differ slightly to those displayed on your screen. Do not worry about this!*

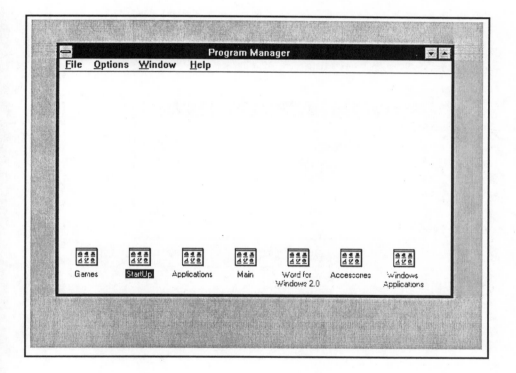

As you can see, the Program Manager window contains a number of icons. There will definitely be icons called **Main, StartUp, Accessories** and **Games**. Depending on how you installed Windows, there may also be icons called **Windows Applications** and **Non-Windows Applications.**

These icons represent groups of programs. A *Group* is essentially an electronic folder where items can be stored together for your convenience.

Restoring or expanding an icon

The simplest way of expanding an icon up to a normal window size (whether the icon represents a group or a program) is to doubleclick the icon.

- Doubleclick the **Games** icon.

☞ *If your doubleclick does not work - it may be a bit slow, or perhaps the mouse moved between the clicks -just try again. If a menu is opened, you can click on the **Restore** option in the menu).*

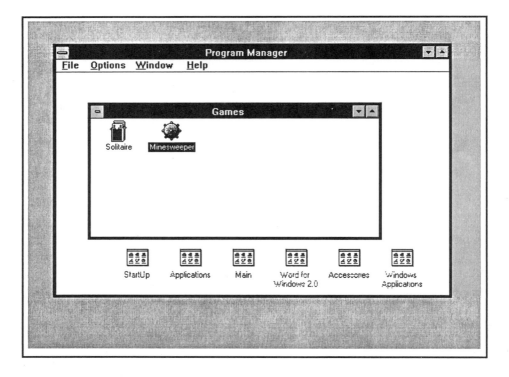

The icon expands to display a window, and you can now see the contents. There are two icons called **Solitaire** and Minesweeper, which represent two games that are supplied with your Windows package.

Minimizing a window

To shrink a window back down to an icon, you simply need to click the
Minimize button in the top right corner of the window.

☞ *When more than one window is open, each window will have its
own Minimize button, so you should make sure you click the
Minimize button for the window you wish to shrink.*

• Click the **Minimize** button on the Games window.

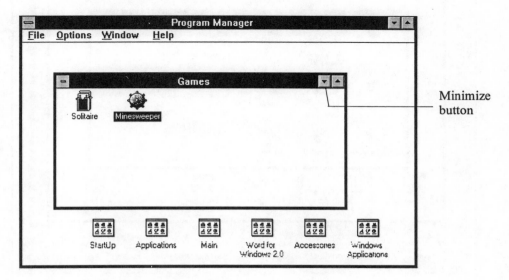

The Games window returns to an icon again.

Remember

Remember the important things so far:

☺ To expand an icon up to a group window, doubleclick the desired
icon.

☺ To shrink a group window back down to an icon, click the window's **Minimize** button.

Starting a program

You will now start one of the programs in the Accessories window. First of all, expand the Accessories window:

• Doubleclick the **Accessories** icon.

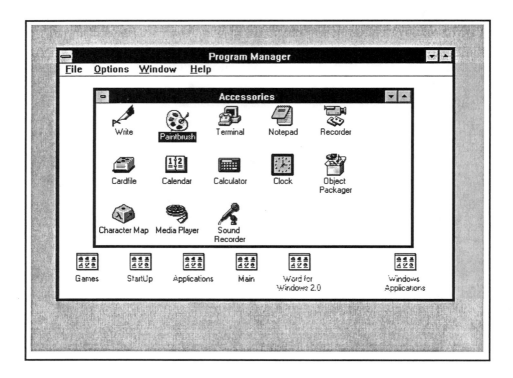

As you can see, the Accessories group contains a collection of programs supplied with your package. This includes Write (a word-processor), Paintbrush, Calendar, Calculator and several other programs. The easiest way to start a program that is represented as an icon is to doubleclick the icon. Just as doubleclicking a group icon opens the group window, so doubleclicking a program icon opens the program.

• Doubleclick the **Write** icon.

A new window is opened for the Write program (see picture on next page). In the normal course of events you would now start typing in a document or would load an existing document, but for now we'll just learn how to exit a program.

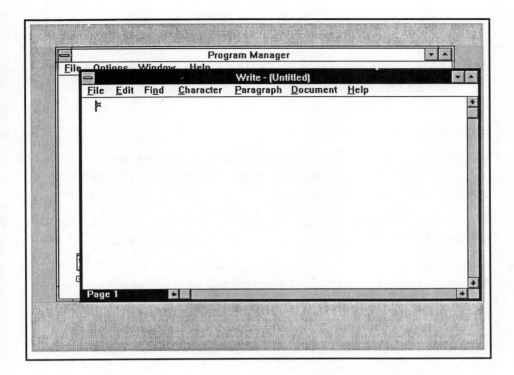

Exiting a program

To exit a program, you can either doubleclick the Control menu in the top left corner of the window, or open the **File** menu and click **Exit**.

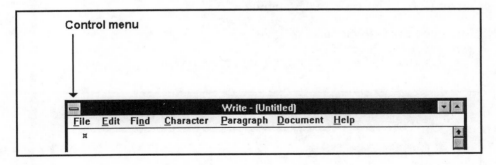

- Doubleclick the Control menu in the Write window (or open the **File** menu and click **Exit**).

The Write window will be closed, and the windows that were behind it will become visible again. Now close the Accessories window.

•   Doubleclick the Control menu of the Accessories window (not the Program Manager window).

Menus

Working with Windows and Windows application programs involves the constant use of menus. You will use menus to start programs, select options, activate features and commands, etc. Happily, they are very easy to use!

The Program Manager Menu bar has four menu headings. **File, Options, Window** and **Help**.

Remember that the idea of the instructions that follow is to help you get familiar with using menus, not to understand what all the options mean!

Opening Menus

There are two ways you can open a menu:

☺   Click on the desired menu heading.

☺   Hold down the **Alt** key, and press the letter that is underlined in the desired menu heading.

Do not worry if you open the wrong menu by mistake. You can either click on the correct one instead, or use the cursor control keys, **ArrowRight** and **ArrowLeft**, to move between menus.

Now open the **File** menu as follows:

•   Click the **File** menu heading (or press **Alt+F**).

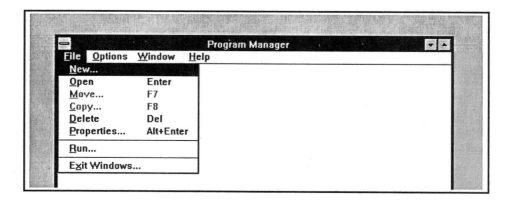

The menu is opened giving you a list of options available, in this case the options relate to files or the icons that represent them.

- Now click the **Options** menu heading (or press the **ArrowRight** key).

The next menu is opened giving a list of options that determine how the group windows will be handled.

- Click the **Window** menu heading (or press the **ArrowRight** key).

You can use the options available in the **Window** menu to control how windows will be arranged on your screen. This time, there will also be a list of the groups currently on your system.

- Click the **Help** menu heading.

You can use this menu to obtain help on the program you are working with. The information will be displayed on your screen. Using Help is described in *Appendix C*.

Closing menus

To close a menu, simply click anywhere other than on a menu (but be careful you don't activate something else by mistake), or press **Esc** twice.

- Press **Esc** twice.

Control menu

Another special menu that is not shown in the menu bar is the Control menu. All the windows in Windows have a Control menu, which you open by clicking the minus sign in the top left corner of the window.

Open the Main group as follows:

- Doubleclick the **Main** group icon.

☞ *There are now TWO different Control menus - the Control menu for the current application, i.e. Program Manager, and the Control menu for the current window, i.e. the Main group window.*

- Click the Control menu on the Main window.

The Control menu contains commands that give you control over the window - e.g. the position and size.

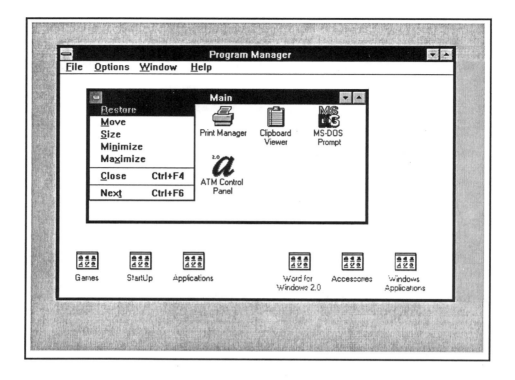

☞ *Some of the menu options may be lighter in colour, which means that they cannot be selected at the moment.*

☞ *For some menu options, you will have noticed that on the right-hand side of the menu there are some key combinations, e.g. **Ctrl+F4** opposite **Close**. These are short cuts which you can use to give commands from the keyboard without having to open the menu.*

• Click on **Close** in the menu to close the window.

• Click the Program Manager window Control menu.

There is only one difference between this menu and the previous one - this time the short-cut to close the window is **Alt+F4**. This lets you distinguish between closing the group window you are working in as opposed to closing the Windows program itself.

• Close the menu by pressing **Esc**.

Selecting an option in a menu

Once you have a menu open, you can either click the desired option, or press the letter that is underlined in the option.

Open the Accessories and Games group windows as follows:

- Doubleclick the **Accessories** icon.

- Doubleclick the **Games** icon.

Close the Games window as follows:

- Open the Games window Control menu (not the Program Manager Control menu!) by clicking it.

- Point at the **Close** option and click.

The window should be closed. When you close a group window, it shrinks back to an icon in the Program Manager window.

- Open the Accessories window Control menu by clicking it.

- Point at the **Close** option and click.

List boxes

Many of the options in Windows menus include a list box, a drop down list from which you can select an item. You will take a look at one now, without using it.

- Doubleclick the **Main** group icon.

- Click the **File** menu - that is **File** in the menu bar, not the icon File Manager that appears in the Main group window.

- Click **Copy** in the menu that is opened.

The following is displayed on your screen:

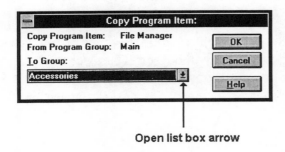

Open list box arrow

To the right of the box containing the word <u>Accessories</u> is a downward pointing arrow that opens the list box. You can scroll through the options in the list box using the up/down arrow keys, or open the list by clicking the open list box arrow.

• Click the **Open list box arrow**.

The list box will open to reveal the options.

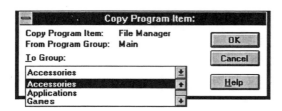

• Click one of the alternatives in the list.

This new value has become the copy destination.

• Press **Esc** or click **Cancel**, to abort the Copy command.

Dialog Boxes

Whenever Windows needs some information from you - for example it may need to know which document to want to open, confirmation of a deletion or whether you want to save a file before exiting - it will open a dialog box.

You will be given detailed instructions on how to use each dialog box at the relevant time, but here is a brief introduction to their general features:

• Open the **Control Panel** by doubleclicking its icon.

• Doubleclick the **Printers** icon.

The Printers dialog box is displayed on your screen (see picture on next page). Note that the actual names in the list of printers will depend on the ones you have installed.

This dialog box contains most of the features you will meet in Windows dialog boxes. These include lists (with or without scroll bars), check boxes, and command buttons. You can point at any of these with your mouse.

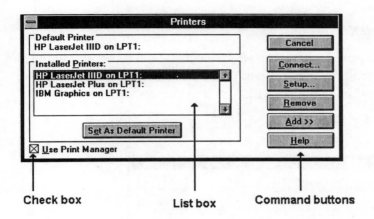

Check box   List box   Command buttons

Check boxes

Check boxes are recognisable by a square box, which may or may not contain a cross, or *check*. They are on/off switches to select a particular option. You can set the switch by clicking on the box.

• Click on the **Use Print Manager** check box.

Note that the check is removed, or added if there was not one before.

☺ If the box IS checked, the option is SELECTED.

☺ If the box IS NOT checked, the option is NOT SELECTED.

• Click on the **Use Print Manager** check box again.

Note that the check is restored, or removed again.

Check boxes are used for options that may be selected if so desired. Sometimes you will have more than one check box and you can select any number of these options, or none at all.

☞ *Note on using the keyboard:*
Pressing the **Spacebar** *will act as a click on the selected check box. Pressing* **Tab** *will select the various buttons and boxes in order.*

Lists

Lists are used where you need to indicate which item you are working with. It is most often a list of files, but on your screen now there is a list of one or more printers. Note that one of the printers in the list will be highlighted.

Selection boxes

Selection boxes are used where you *must* select one out of several options. They are recognisable by the group of circles, one of which will contain a black dot. Clicking on an option will switch to that option.

- Click the **SetUp** button.

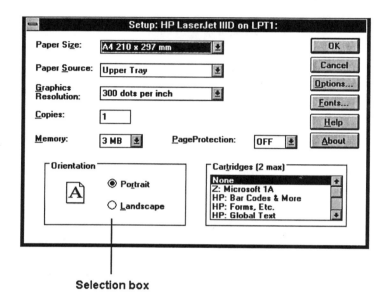

Selection box

The Orientation box contains two such selections - **Portrait** and **Landscape**. The page, of course, must be one of these, but cannot be both or none.

- Click the **Landscape** option circle to select it.

- Click the **Portrait** option circle to select it.

- Click **Cancel** to return to the previous window without saving any changes.

Command Buttons

Every dialog box has an **OK** or **Yes** button, which you can click to complete the settings or alterations you have made. Most boxes also have a **Cancel** button, which enables you to abandon the changes you have made. The current dialog box has some extra buttons - clicking these will open further dialogs.

The **Esc** key also works as a **Cancel** or **Close** button.

• Click the **Close** button.

The Printers dialog box is closed, and any alterations you made are lost.

Finally, close the Control Panel window and Main group window.

• Doubleclick the Control menu of the Control Panel window.

• Doubleclick the Control menu of the Main group window.

Note about the Save Settings on Exit option

It is possible to exit Windows with one or more windows open or just the Program Manager window as you have done so far. If the **Save Settings on Exit** option in the **Options** menu is selected, Windows records which group windows are open when you exit, and next time you start Windows it will open these windows for you. Quite simply, it remembers the state it was in on closing.

If you turn this option off, Windows will always start up as it did the last time the changes were saved. So, if you find a set-up you do like (e.g. always having the Paintbrush Accessories window open), exit Windows with the **Save Settings on Exit** option selected, to record the set-up. Then open Windows and turn the **Save Settings on Exit** option off.

See picture on next page!

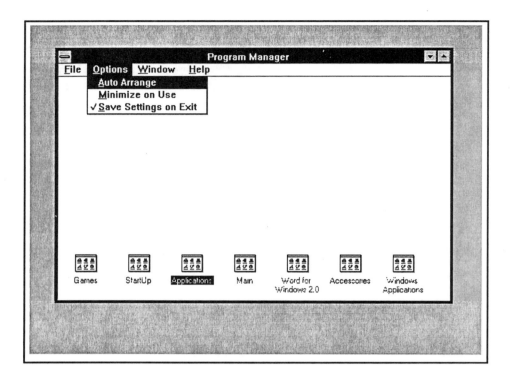

Don't worry about this setting just now.

☺ To toggle the setting on and off, just click on the **Save Settings on Exit** option - the tick, or *check mark*, means it is selected, no check mark means it is not selected.

Exiting Windows

Exiting Windows is equivalent to exiting Program Manager. Once again, the simplest method is to doubleclick the Control menu.

• Doubleclick the Control menu of the Program Manager window.

You are now asked to confirm that you wish to exit Windows.

• Click **OK**.

Your Keyboard Explained

When confronted with a computer keyboard for the first time, novices are often frightened by the many keys other than the normal typewriter keys. The mysterious symbols and the complexity of the keyboard, do require some explanation. This chapter describes the functions of some important individual keys with which you may not be familiar.

Different keyboards

Although there are several different keyboard models, there are two main layouts. One has a group of 10 keys, marked **F1-F10**, on the left-hand side, while the other has the same group of keys **F1-F12** in a row at the top of the keyboard. Virtually all newer systems will have the second type.

Alpha numerical keys and Shift

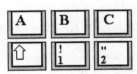

These keys are the normal letter and number keys, as for a standard typewriter. Upper case letters and the characters over the numbers are obtained by using the **Shift** key - shown here, bottom left.

Combined numerical key pad and cursor movement keys

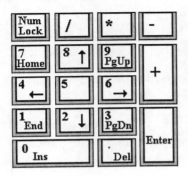

These keys can function in two ways, depending on the state of the Number Lock function. By pressing the **NumLock** key, the **NumLock** indicator will be turned on and off.

Num Lock indicator on
With NumLock lamp lit, these keys will work as number keys.

Num Lock indicator off
With NumLock lamp not lit, these keys will work as cursor movement keys. Just how, and if, they work, will depend on the program you are running. A word processor, for example, will almost certainly use the keys to move the cursor around in a text.

Separate cursor movement keys

Some keyboards will have a separate group of keys dedicated to cursor movement. Just how, and if, they work, will depend on the program you are running.

Home. This key is often used to move the cursor to the beginning of a line, screen display, or text.

End. This key is often used to move the cursor to the end of a line, screen display, or text.

Page Up. This key is often used to move the cursor to the beginning of a screen display, or text.

Page Down. This key is often used to move the cursor to the end of screen display, or text.

Insert. This key is often used to control how new text is inserted into a text. Pressing the key will often toggle between an insert and overwrite mode. Insert means that text will be inserted at the cursor's position and the following text moved over. The overwrite mode will cause text entered at the cursor's position to replace that which already exists.

Delete. This key is often used to delete the character at the cursor's position.

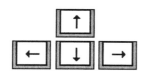

The Arrow keys. These keys are most often used to move the cursor one position in the indicated direction.

Function keys

The function keys are grouped on the left-hand side of the keyboard (**F1-F10**), or in a row at the top of it (**F1-F12**).

These keys are used by application programs, and will be assigned different functions for each program, and sometimes different functions at different points within the same program. Think of these as "short cut" keys, since they're usually used to let one keystroke do the job of many.

For example, **F1** could be defined to save a text in a word processor program, to show a help text in a communications program, or to delete an entry in a database program. In each case, without the use of the function key, you might have to perform several different commands to make the program do what you want.

Special keys

This section is dedicated to some keys with a special importance.

Enter key

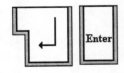

The **Enter** key is perhaps the most important key of all. It is mainly used in two ways.

When typing in commands, instructions, and data, you usually have to press this key to confirm your input. In such cases, although you may have typed in a command, it is not followed until you have pressed the **Enter** key.

A word processor program will require you to press the **Enter** key to mark the end of a paragraph, and move the cursor down to the next line. This is similar to the CR (Carriage Return) key of a standard typewriter.

Backspace key

The **Backspace** key is normally used to delete the character immediately to the left of the cursor.

Caps Lock key

 This key is used to lock the alphabetical keys, **A-Z**, to their upper-cases, as for a standard typewriter.

Ctrl key

 The **Ctrl** key (short for Control) is used together with other keys, to perform special operations in an application program.

Alt key

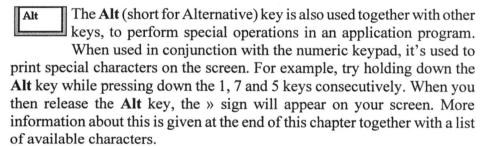 The **Alt** (short for Alternative) key is also used together with other keys, to perform special operations in an application program.

When used in conjunction with the numeric keypad, it's used to print special characters on the screen. For example, try holding down the **Alt** key while pressing down the 1, 7 and 5 keys consecutively. When you then release the **Alt** key, the » sign will appear on your screen. More information about this is given at the end of this chapter together with a list of available characters.

Esc key

 The **Esc** key (short for Escape) is usually used in application programs to exit a part of that program or to undo a change you have made.

Tab key

 This key is normally used to jump between pre-defined margin positions, or between input fields.

Print Screen key

This key will result in a copy of the screen display being sent to the printer for printing, or when using Windows, the copy being sent to the Clipboard.

More about your keyboard

The keyboard has its own small *buffer*, or memory, to store up to 11 key strokes. These will be held until the computer is ready to print them on the screen. If this buffer gets filled, which usually happens when the computer is doing a lot of processing and doesn't have time to check for keyboard inputs as frequently as it normally does, the computer will beep. This tells you that no more information can currently be received from the keyboard. If you're a very fast typist and you're using a program that slows up keyboard input (communications programs are famous for this), there are several programs that can increase the buffer's size so that you won't have to wait for your computer to catch up to you.

It is also possible that keys will have an auto-repeat function. This means that if you keep a key depressed, the computer will see this as if you are repeatedly pressing that key.

Producing graphics characters with the Alt key

Your computer is not only capable of producing letters and numbers, it can also produce many graphic characters. These characters can be used with certain programs, for example, to create boxes and lines.

To write these characters, which are not displayed on any of the keys on your keyboard, you need to press the **Alt** key, in conjunction with a number code, using the number keys on the right-hand side of the keyboard.

To obtain a character in the table, you must look up its ASCII number code. The example below will type an Ä character.

- Hold down the **Alt** key.

- Type in the code number for the desired character, using the number key pad on the right-hand side of the keyboard, for example:

  142

- Release the **Alt** key.

☞ *This will not necessarily work for all programs or printers, since some use their own character sets. In such cases, you should consult the appropriate manual.*

The ASCII Table shows the number and corresponding character of the IBM character set. These are the characters you can print using the **Alt** key.

The ASCII table

21 = §	69 = E	107 = k	145 = æ	183 = ╖	221 = ▌
32 =	70 = F	108 = l	146 = Æ	184 = ╕	222 = ▐
33 = !	71 = G	109 = m	147 = ô	185 = ╣	223 = ▀
34 = "	72 = H	110 = n	148 = ö	186 = ║	224 = α
35 = #	73 = I	111 = o	149 = ò	187 = ╗	225 = β
36 = %	74 = J	112 = p	150 = û	188 = ╝	226 = Γ
37 =	75 = K	113 = q	151 = ù	189 = ╜	227 = π
38 = &	76 = L	114 = r	152 = ÿ	190 = ╛	228 = Σ
39 = '	77 = M	115 = s	153 = Ö	191 = ┐	229 = σ
40 = (	78 = N	116 = t	154 = Ü	192 = └	230 = µ
41 =)	79 = O	117 = u	155 = ¢	193 = ┴	231 = τ
42 = *	80 = P	118 = v	156 =	194 = ┬	232 = Φ
43 = +	81 = Q	119 = w	157 = ¥	195 = ├	233 = Θ
44 = ,	82 = R	120 = x	158 = ₧	196 = ─	234 = Ω
45 = —	83 = S	121 = y	159 = ƒ	197 = ┼	235 = δ
46 = .	84 = T	122 = z	160 = á	198 = ╞	236 = ∞
47 = /	85 = U	123 = {	161 = í	199 = ╟	237 = ø
48 = 0	86 = V	124 = ¦	162 = ó	200 = ╚	238 = ∈
49 = 1	87 = W	125 = }	163 = ú	201 = ╔	239 = ∩
50 = 2	88 = X	126 = ~	164 = ñ	202 = ╩	240 = ≡
51 = 3	89 = Y	127 = ⌂	165 = Ñ	203 = ╦	241 = ±
52 = 4	90 = Z	128 = Ç	166 = ª	204 = ╠	242 = ≥
53 = 5	91 = [	129 = ü	167 = º	205 = ═	243 = ≤
54 = 6	92 = \	130 = é	168 = ¿	206 = ╬	244 = ⌠
55 = 7	93 =]	131 = â	169 = ⌐	207 = ╧	245 = ⌡
56 = 8	94 = ^	132 = ä	170 = ¬	208 = ╨	246 = ÷
57 = 9	95 = _	133 = à	171 = ½	209 = ╤	247 = ≈
58 = :	96 = `	134 = å	172 = ¼	210 = ╥	248 = °
59 = ;	97 = a	135 = ç	173 = ¡	211 = ╙	249 = ●
60 = <	98 = b	136 = ê	174 = «	212 = ╘	250 = ·
61 = =	99 = c	137 = ë	175 = »	213 = ╒	251 = √
62 = >	100 = d	138 = è	176 = ░	214 = ╓	252 = ⁿ
63 = ?	101 = e	139 = ï	177 = ▒	215 = ╫	253 = ²
64 = @	102 = f	140 = î	178 = ▓	216 = ╪	254 = ■
65 = A	103 = g	141 = ì	179 = │	217 = ┘	255 =
66 = B	104 = h	142 = Ä	180 = ┤	218 = ┌	
67 = C	105 = i	143 = Å	181 = ╡	219 = █	
68 = D	106 = j	144 = É	182 = ╢	220 = ▄	

Using Help

Most Windows windows have a Help menu and a short cut key **F1** to open the help program. If you open the Help menu and select one of the options, a Help window will be opened containing information about the topic you selected.

Although the following instructions are specific to Program Manager, the procedures apply to any Windows program.

* Open the **Help** menu and select **Contents** (or press **F1**).

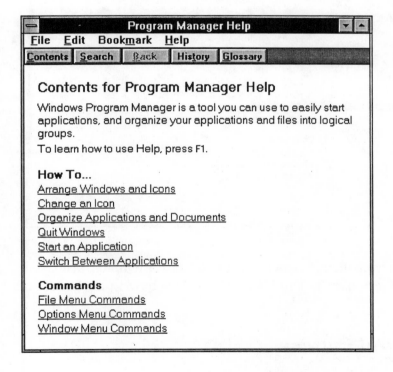

Since you are currently using Program Manager, the help options relate to Program Manager.

* Click one of the topics.

A new window is opened, with an index of topics relating to the selected topic. You can point at a topic with the mouse and click. You will know when you are pointing at a topic that has further information available because the mouse pointer changes to a hand.

- Experiment with the topics available - an example screen is shown below.

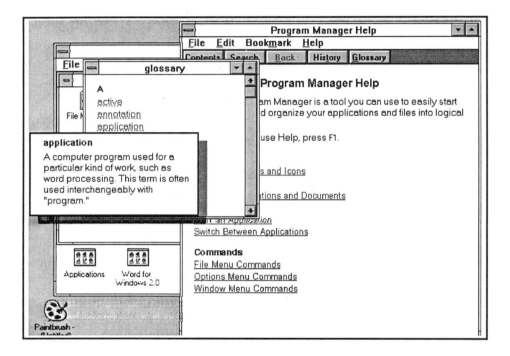

A list of keys and their functions in dialog boxes will be displayed. Remember you can use the scroll bars to see items beyond the bottom of the screen.

Help control buttons

At the top of the window under the menu bar there are five buttons that you can use to move around the help information.

Browse buttons (<< and >>)

The **Browse** buttons are used to move one topic along. The options the either side of Dialog Box Keys in the index were Editing Keys and Cursor Movement Keys.

- Experiment by clicking the **Browse** buttons.

Back button

Quite often when you are looking through a Help file, you will want to get back to something you saw on a previous screen, but will not quite be able to remember how you got there!

The **Back** button takes you back one step at a time through the commands you have given since starting Help, including referencing different topics using the hand pointer.

- Experiment by clicking the **Back**.

You will eventually reach the point at which you entered the Help system, and cannot backtrack any further.

History

A list of Help windows you have opened is recorded in a list.

- Click the **History** button and select a topic.

Index

You can call up the Help index at any time by clicking the **Index** button.

- Click the **Index** button.

You are returned to the top-level index, and can select from Program Manager Keys (that you have just been using) or general Windows keys.

Searching

You can search for a particular topic using the **Search** button.

- Click the **Search** button.
- Select the topic you are looking for from the list, for example, <u>arranging icons</u>.

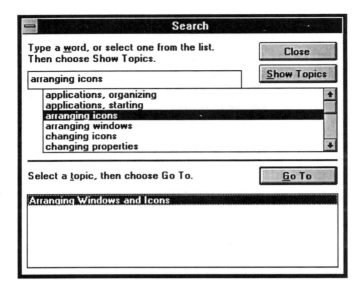

- Click the **Show Topics** button.

- Click **Go To** to actually view the topic.

Printing out a help file

☺ To print the current help topic, open the **File** menu and select **Print Topic**.

Exiting from Help

You exit from a Help window in the same manner as any other application window.

- Select **File, Exit,** or doubleclick the Help window Control menu.

Selecting a Printer

This Appendix gives you general information about selecting a printer when using a Windows application. The pictures are taken from Word for Windows v6, but apply in general terms to most applications.

Selecting a printer

If you have more than one printer installed, you can easily select the desired printer.

- Select **File**, **Print** (or **Print Setup** in many applications).

- Click the **Printer** button.

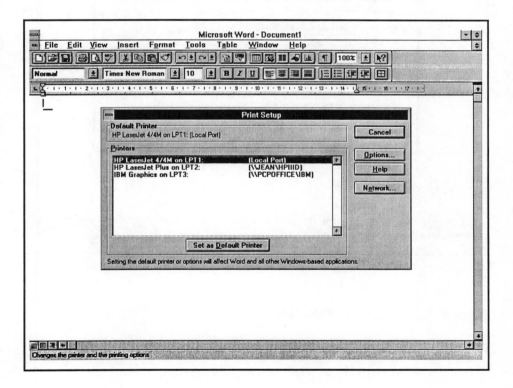

- Doubleclick the desired printer from the list of printers then click **Close**.

Changing a printer setup

It is possible to make some changes to the printers you have installed. You will now investigate this without making any changes.

- Select **File**, **Print**.

- Click **Printer**.

- Click **Options**.

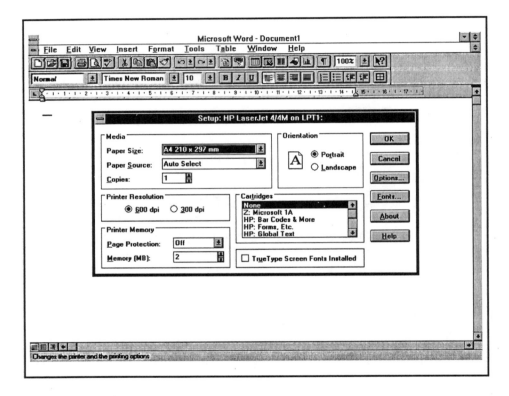

Look at the settings available, and make the desired changes.

- You can usually click **Cancel** to abandon changes.

- Click **Close** or **OK** to confirm your changes.

Index

Index

Free exercise diskette

There is a diskette which accompanies this book that contains the original files and programs needed to fully follow the exercises in this book.

The exercise diskette should be attached to the inside back cover.

If the diskette is missing, you can obtain one from *PC Productions Limited* as follows:

> fax PC Productions on **0453-755400**

or,

> write to:
>
> **PC Productions Limited**
> **PCCR Word for Windows v6 diskette**
> **Kendrick Hall**
> **Kendrick Street**
> **STROUD**
> **GL5 1AA**

When requesting the diskette, <u>proof of purchase</u> will be needed. Ask for the **PCCR Word for Windows v6** diskette. Unless you say otherwise, you will be sent a 3.5" diskette.